Backbone.js Patterns and Best Practices

A one-stop guide to best practices and design patterns when building applications using Backbone.js

Swarnendu De

BIRMINGHAM - MUMBAI

Backbone.js Patterns and Best Practices

First published: January 2014

Production Reference: 1200114

Published by Packt Publishing Ltd.
Livery Place
35 Livery Street
Birmingham B3 2PB, UK.

ISBN 978-1-78328-357-6

www.packtpub.com

Cover Image by Manali Mandal (mandal.manali@gmail.com)

Credits

Author
Swarnendu De

Reviewers
Marc D. Bodley
Florian Bruniaux
Philippe Charrière
Ezekiel Chentnik
Lorenzo Pisani

Acquisition Editors
Mary Jasmine Nadar
Gregory Wild

Lead Technical Editor
Ruchita Bhansali

Technical Editors
Vrinda Amberkar Bhosale
Shubhangi H. Dhamgaye
Shweta Pant
Ritika Singh

Copy Editors
Janbal Dharmaraj
Sayanee Mukherjee

Project Coordinator
Sageer Parkar

Proofreader
Ameesha Green

Indexer
Hemangini Bari

Graphics
Abhinash Sahu

Production Coordinator
Arvindkumar Gupta

Cover Work
Arvindkumar Gupta

About the Author

Swarnendu De is the director of Innofied Solution Pvt. Ltd. (`http://www.innofied.com`), a specialized mobile, web, and game development company. He manages technical operations and leads the JavaScript development team there. For the last seven years, he has been working with numerous JavaScript technologies including Backbone.js, Node.js, ExtJS, Sencha, and so on, and has developed more than 50 complex JavaScript-based applications thus far. He regularly writes at his personal blog, company blog, and the Tuts+ network. He has been working with Backbone.js for the last 2 years and has developed multiple, large, and complex Backbone.js-based applications using this technology.

Swarnendu lives in Kolkata—the city of joy. He loves travelling, photography, and spending time with his family. You can reach him through his website at `http://www.swarnendude.com` or via Twitter at `@swarnendude`.

Acknowledgments

Writing such a book is quite hard, especially when you are busy managing the operations and technical team at your own startup. I would like to thank my business partner, Sandip Saha, who shared the workload so that I could spend more time completing this book. Special thanks to my senior, Saikat Sengupta, who did all the editing and proofreading for each chapter—the whole journey wouldn't have been this smooth without his help.

Writing this book would never have been possible without the help of the Backbone community who have contributed to all the technologies that I have used in this book. I would like to extend my heartfelt gratitude to the forums, tutorials, and blog posts for all the discussions, ideas, and feedback that shaped this book. I would like to thank the technical reviewers who provided immensely useful feedback that helped me enrich the content of this book. I am very much thankful to Sageer Parkar, the project coordinator of this book, for his cooperation and assistance.

I want to thank my brother, my closest friends Subhradip, Sudipta, Priyendra, Suramya, Arup, Payel, and the entire Innofied team for all their support. Finally, a special thank you to my lovely wife for the moral support and the amazing cover page photo.

About the Reviewers

Marc D. Bodley is a passionate user experience engineer and a jack-of-all-trades developer, with over 8 years experience with JavaScript and frontend technology. He is excited to see JavaScript being adopted as more of a mainstream development language and not just an accessory to development. He is equally excited to see the structure and thought process of more conventional, strongly typed languages being applied to JavaScript, to bring order to what is potentially a large and disorganized JS-driven code base. He has worked on large- and small-scale applications for a range of organizations, from Belk.com to start-up style data-heavy applications. He continues to look for, learn ,and enforce JavaScript and programming practices, and was grateful to be a contributor to this effort.

Florian Bruniaux is a French student of the University of Technology of Troyes (UTT), in the IT and Information Systems department. He is passionate about new technology, particularly process optimization and software development.

He specializes in frontend and client-side development, and has worked for various companies such as Aylan (a French startup), Oxylane, and EDF where he participated in IT projects such as server monitoring systems, cross-browsers, or multidevice app conception and development.

I would like to thank Steve Burghgraeve, IT engineer at Oxylane, and Aurélien Bénel, teacher-researcher and lecturer in Computer Science at UTT, for their help in my different projects and all the knowledge they've transferred to me.

Philippe Charrière is a bid manager at Steria in France. At night, he is an open source developer advocate at Golo project (`http://golo-lang.org/`) and a Backbone enthusiast. He wrote a small open source book in French about Backbone.js (`https://github.com/k33g/backbone.en.douceur/`). He's also an occasional speaker on Backbone.js and mobile technologies. He focuses primarily on open web technologies (front- and server-side).

Ezekiel Chentnik has over 8 years experience in frontend engineering and JavaScript development. He is a JavaScript whiz kid and whatever the challenge is, he takes it. He is passionate about his work and is constantly pushing the limit. His recent projects include some of his favorite JavaScript libraries: Zepto.js, Backbone.js, Underscore.js, Marionette.js, and Modernizr.js. Learn more about Ezekiel at `http://ezekielchentnik.com`.

Lorenzo Pisani is a software engineer with over a decade of experience developing applications with PHP, MySQL, and JavaScript. As a huge advocate of open source software, he publishes just about everything he builds outside of work to his GitHub profile (`https://github.com/Zeelot`) for others to use and learn from.

www.PacktPub.com

Support files, eBooks, discount offers and more

You might want to visit www.PacktPub.com for support files and downloads related to your book.

Did you know that Packt offers eBook versions of every book published, with PDF and ePub files available? You can upgrade to the eBook version at www.PacktPub.com and as a print book customer, you are entitled to a discount on the eBook copy. Get in touch with us at service@packtpub.com for more details.

At www.PacktPub.com, you can also read a collection of free technical articles, sign up for a range of free newsletters and receive exclusive discounts and offers on Packt books and eBooks.

http://PacktLib.PacktPub.com

Do you need instant solutions to your IT questions? PacktLib is Packt's online digital book library. Here, you can access, read and search across Packt's entire library of books.

Why Subscribe?

- Fully searchable across every book published by Packt
- Copy and paste, print and bookmark content
- On demand and accessible via web browser

Free Access for Packt account holders

If you have an account with Packt at www.PacktPub.com, you can use this to access PacktLib today and view nine entirely free books. Simply use your login credentials for immediate access.

Dedicated to my parents.

*All the good that happened in my life happened because of your example,
guidance, and love!*

Table of Contents

Preface

Though Backbone.js provides a structure for JavaScript applications, developers need to take care of most of the design patterns and best practices themselves. Over the years, my JavaScript development team and I worked on multiple Backbone.js applications ranging from simple to extremely complex. We experienced different types of problems related to layout management, project architecture, modular development, and so on. Before I started writing this book, I spent a significant amount of time trying to figure out solutions for all the common problems associated with the development of Backbone.js applications. In this book, I have documented all my findings in detail.

Whether you are an intermediate- or advanced-level Backbone.js developer, this book will guide you through the best practices and patterns to handle different issues with each Backbone component. Whether this is by using your own solution or an existing Backbone plugin, you will get a clear idea of the best way to resolve any problem.

Instead of developing a single application spanning all the chapters, a simple and complete example on each topic is provided separately throughout this book. This is because it would be quite difficult to implement all the tips and patterns given in this book in a single application. Moreover, we preferred to provide immediate and compact solutions to problems, instead of including all the problems and solutions in a single large application. Within a short span, this book tries to cover all the important points you may need for the development of your Backbone.js application.

What this book covers

Chapter 1, Reducing Boilerplate with Plugin Development, starts with the basics of why reusing your code is important, and how we can achieve that by creating custom Backbone.js widgets and mixins.

Chapter 2, Working with Views, discusses the different points related to view rendering and layout management. Starting from partial updating of views, functionality of nested views or subviews for different processes of JavaScript template management and best practices, this chapter covers most of the problems a developer may face while working with views. We conclude by writing about the Marionette custom views and the Layout Manager plugin for complex app layout management.

Chapter 3, Working with Models, talks about different patterns while working with Backbone models, including data validation, model serialization to fetch data, and saving data to the server. We also analyze the relational data model for one-to-many and many-to-many relationships using Backbone's relational plugin.

Chapter 4, Working with Collections, covers a number of common problems that developers face while using Backbone collections. We explain how to apply basic and multiple sorting, how to apply filtering to a collection, and how to manage a collection while a mixed set of data is passed from the server.

Chapter 5, Routing Best Practices and Subrouting, covers a number of best practices you should follow while working with routers. We also discuss the benefits of using multiple routers or subrouters for complex and large-level applications.

Chapter 6, Working with Events, Sync, and Storage, begins by describing the importance of custom events to enhance an application's modularity and reusability. We also discuss using an application-level event manager to work as a centralized PubSub system, and the use of the `Backbone.sync()` method to create different data-persistent strategies.

Chapter 7, Organizing Backbone Applications – Structure, Optimize, and Deploy, is one of the most important chapters that a developer will find very useful if they are developing a complex Backbone application. It talks about the application directory structure, organizing and managing files with RequireJS, and the different architectural patterns that every JavaScript developer should follow to develop large-scale application architectures.

Chapter 8, Unit Test, Stub, Spy, and Mock Your App, talks about the benefits of unit testing your JavaScript application, and introduces you to the QUnit and SinonJS test frameworks.

Appendix A, Books, Tutorials, and References, lists a number of useful Backbone.js resources that you may find helpful.

Appendix B, Precompiling Templates on the Server Side, describes the benefits of precompiling JavaScript templates at server side with examples.

Appendix C, Organizing Templates with AMD and Require.js, discusses the process of storing and organizing JavaScript templates with the RequireJS, text!, and tpl! plugins.

What you need for this book

Most of the code in this book can be opened in a simple text editor (Notepad++ or Sublime Text). To run the code, you can use any web browser. For some code, you may need a local server (Apache or IIS) to be set up. For Node.js-related functionality, you need to set up a Node.js server.

Who this book is for

This book is for any developers who has a basic knowledge of Backbone.js and is looking for solutions to common Backbone.js problems, looking to enforce reusability in their code by removing boilerplate and developing custom plugins and extensions, and hoping to use the most effective patterns to develop large-scale web application architecture.

This book is not a general introduction to Backbone.js or JavaScript design patterns. There are lots of books, tutorials, and screencasts available that cover a general introduction in great detail. While this book will discuss the basics of the Backbone.js components in each chapter, the main priority will be to provide you with the concepts of developing a robust, high quality, and flexible code base.

Conventions

In this book, you will find a number of styles of text that distinguish between different kinds of information. Here are some examples of these styles, and an explanation of their meaning.

Code words in text, database table names, folder names, filenames, file extensions, pathnames, dummy URLs, user input, and Twitter handles are shown as follows: "We can include other contexts through the use of the include directive."

A block of code is set as follows:

```
var MainView = Backbone.View.extend({
  el : '#main',
  render : function(){
    this.$el.html(new BaseView().render().el);
  }
});
```

When we wish to draw your attention to a particular part of a code block, the relevant lines or items are set in bold:

```
var BaseView = Backbone.View.extend({
  template : '<h1><%= name %></h1>',
  render : function(){
    var html = _.template(this.template, {
      name : 'Swarnendu De'
    });
    this.$el.html(html);
    return this;
  }
});
```

New terms and **important words** are shown in bold. Words that you see on the screen, for example, in menus or dialog boxes appear in the text like this: "clicking on the **Next** button moves you to the next screen".

 Warnings or important notes appear in a box like this.

 Tips and tricks appear like this.

Reader feedback

Feedback from our readers is always welcome. Let us know what you think about this book—what you liked or may have disliked. Reader feedback is important for us to develop titles that you really get the most out of.

To send us general feedback, simply send an e-mail to feedback@packtpub.com, and mention the book title via the subject of your message.

If there is a topic that you have expertise in and you are interested in either writing or contributing to a book, see our author guide on www.packtpub.com/authors.

Customer support

Now that you are the proud owner of a Packt book, we have a number of things to help you to get the most from your purchase.

Downloading the example code

You can download the example code files for all Packt books you have purchased from your account at http://www.packtpub.com. If you purchased this book elsewhere, you can visit http://www.packtpub.com/support and register to have the files e-mailed directly to you.

Errata

Although we have taken every care to ensure the accuracy of our content, mistakes do happen. If you find a mistake in one of our books—maybe a mistake in the text or the code—we would be grateful if you would report this to us. By doing so, you can save other readers from frustration and help us improve subsequent versions of this book. If you find any errata, please report them by visiting http://www.packtpub.com/submit-errata, selecting your book, clicking on the **errata submission form** link, and entering the details of your errata. Once your errata are verified, your submission will be accepted and the errata will be uploaded on our website, or added to any list of existing errata, under the Errata section of that title. Any existing errata can be viewed by selecting your title from http://www.packtpub.com/support.

Piracy

Piracy of copyright material on the Internet is an ongoing problem across all media. At Packt, we take the protection of our copyright and licenses very seriously. If you come across any illegal copies of our works, in any form, on the Internet, please provide us with the location address or website name immediately so that we can pursue a remedy.

Please contact us at copyright@packtpub.com with a link to the suspected pirated material.

We appreciate your help in protecting our authors, and our ability to bring you valuable content.

Questions

You can contact us at questions@packtpub.com if you are having a problem with any aspect of the book, and we will do our best to address it.

1
Reducing Boilerplate with Plugin Development

"When working on a web application that involves a lot of JavaScript, one of the first things you learn is to stop tying your data to the DOM. It's all too easy to create JavaScript applications that end up as tangled piles of jQuery selectors and callbacks, all trying frantically to keep data in sync between the HTML UI, your JavaScript logic, and the database on your server. For rich client-side applications, a more structured approach is often helpful."

The previous excerpt from `http://backbonejs.org` precisely specifies the problem that Backbone.js solves. Backbone.js provides a way to simplify the JavaScript application structure, which was clearly a nightmare, even a few years ago. Today, we have moved a long way from tightly coupled jQuery-based applications to heavy frontend applications, and a major portion of the application logic now relies on the UI part. This means organizing the application structure is now one of the most significant aspects of application development, and should take care of the reusability, modularity, and testability of the components of an application.

Being an extremely lightweight library, Backbone.js, along with the utility library Underscore.js, provides a set of tools that help to organize your code and makes it easier to develop single-page web applications. Backbone delivers a minimalistic solution to separate the concerns of your application; features include RESTful operations, persistent strategies, models, views with logic, event-driven component communication, templating, and routing facilities. Its simplistic nature, excellent documentation, and a large community of developers make it easy to learn how to use this library.

However, to develop a robust system, we do not depend only on the basic functional components of the framework; we have to use many other libraries, plugins, and reusable add-ons to support the core system as well. While Backbone.js with its core components provides a way to structure your application at the base level, it is really not enough until we either develop our own or use other open source extensions, plugins, and useful patterns. In order to create solid, software architecture, we need to make the best use of existing components and follow proper design patterns. This is what we intend to deliver in this book.

This is not a general introduction book, and we expect our readers to have a basic understanding of the Backbone.js framework. If you are a beginner and looking for good resources to start with Backbone.js, we will recommend you to refer *Appendix A, Books, Tutorials, and References*, of this book, where we listed a number of useful resources to help you master Backbone.js.

We will start with an understanding of how we can re-use our code and reduce a boilerplate by developing custom extensions, plugins, and mixins. In the latter chapters, we will start discussing the common problems, tips, patterns, best practices, and open source plugins for each Backbone.js component. We will also see how we can use Backbone.js to structure and architect complex web applications, and understand the basics of unit testing in JavaScript-based applications. In addition, instead of developing a single application spanning all the chapters, we have tried to provide simple and complete examples on each topic separately throughout this book. In this chapter, we will learn a few important topics with examples. These topics and concepts will be used many times in rest of the chapters. They are as follows:

- **Basic components of Backbone.js**: This consists of a brief discussion about the definitions of the Backbone components

- **Use of Underscore.js**: This consists of a brief discussion about Underscore.js and the utility of using this library for JavaScript-based projects

- **Re-use code with extensions**: This consists of reusing the Backbone code by moving common code blocks to parent-level classes

- **Backbone mixins**: This consists of an explanation of what mixin is, and how and where to use mixins with Backbone

Basic components of Backbone.js

We will look into some basic concepts of Backbone.js and Underscore.js before moving to the plugin development section. Backbone.js is a client-side MV* framework that provides a set of tools and building blocks required to structure a JavaScript application. Important tools that Backbone.js offers are as follows:

- `Backbone.Model`: Models are the entity of an application that store data and contain some logic around data such as validation, conversion, and data interaction.

- `Backbone.View`: Views present an idea of organizing your **Document Object Model (DOM)** interface into logical blocks, and represent the model and collection data in them. Views are excellent tools to organize all the JavaScript event handlers and to add dynamic HTML content in your application via optional use of JavaScript templates. As Backbone follows an MV* pattern, Backbone views mostly work as presenters and take care of the major portion of application functionality.

- `Backbone.Collection`: A collection is a group of models. A collection includes a lot of functionality as well as Underscore utility methods to help you work on multiple data models.

- `Backbone.Router`: A router provides methods for routing client-side pages and acts subsequently whenever there is a change in the browser's URL. A router maintains the application state as per the URL change.

- `Backbone.Events`: Events are an important concept in Backbone, since they provide a mechanism to use the PubSub pattern and decouple your application components.

Apart from these, there are other tools such as `Backbone.History`, which manages the browser history and the back/forward buttons in accordance with the routers. Also, we have `Backbone.Sync`, which is a single method that provides a nice abstraction to the network access through Backbone models and collections.

Using Underscore.js

Underscore.js (http://underscorejs.org/) is a powerful utility library that provides a lot of functional programming support for your JavaScript code. In general, JavaScript comes up with a very low number of utility methods on its own, and most of the time we need to either develop our own functions or depend on another library for these methods. Underscore comes up with a bagful of highly efficient utility methods, which makes it an excellent tool for your JavaScript projects. The functions it provides can be grouped into the following sections:

- Collections (Array or Object)
- Arrays
- Functions
- Objects
- Utility
- Chaining

These include functions for iterations, sorting, filtering, conversions, templating, comparisons, scope binding, and many more. The main benefits of using this small library are as follows:

- It helps you to make the JavaScript code more intuitive and concise.

- In addition to the convenient methods, Underscore also implements cross-browser versions of newer JavaScript functions, which are only available in modern browsers. Underscore will detect whether the browser supports the method, and will use the native implementation if it is present. This boosts the function's performance to a great extent.

- The minified and gzipped version of the library weighs only 4.9 KB, which leaves little excuse for not taking advantages of this library.

- The library is completely DOM-free—so you can use it for your server-side JavaScript code as well.

- Excellent documentation similar to Backbone.js with examples is available at http://underscorejs.org/.

Backbone.js has a hard dependency on Underscore.js, and you are bound to use it if you are developing your applications with Backbone.js. However, even when you are not using Backbone, we encourage you to use Underscore.js for your JavaScript projects. It adds no overhead, integrates easily, and makes your code more robust even when you are not aware of all the underlying engineering principles employed by this library.

There is another library named `Lo-dash` (`http://lodash.com`), which provides an Underscore built to perform drop-in replacement of the Underscore.js library. It is said to have a slightly better performance than Underscore.js. You can try either of them to achieve the same result.

Re-using code with extensions

Backbone is quite a small library in comparison with other libraries. Any complex application can be structured and developed with Backbone, but the framework itself doesn't come with prebuilt widgets or reusable UI components. In this section, we will talk about some Backbone and JavaScript techniques that will help you build a reusable interface library.

For simple and small applications, code reusability doesn't always seem much of a necessity. But as you proceed to create an application with multiple views, models, and collections, you find that a certain portion of your code gets repeated several times. Creating reusable extensions and plugins in such cases improves the performance of the application by enhancing modularity and reducing the code size. Let's create a simple Backbone view to understand how we can create an extension, shown in the following code snippet:

```javascript
var User = Backbone.Model.extend({
  defaults: {
    name: 'John Doe'
  }
});

var UserItemView = Backbone.View.extend({
  template: '<span><%= name %></span>',
  render: function () {
    var tpl = _.template(this.template),
      html = tpl(this.model.toJSON());

    this.$el.html(html);
    return this;
  }
});

// Create a view instance passing a new model instance
var userItem = new UserItemView({
  model: new User
});

$(document.body).append(userItem.render().el);
```

The view named `UserItemView` is a simple Backbone view where we want to display our model data inside a template and append this view element to the DOM. This is a fundamental functionality of Backbone where the primary requirement is to display a model's data as a view. If we have another similar view with a model, and this has the same functionality, the `render()` function will also be identical. That said, won't it be beneficial if we move the common code to a base class and extend that class to inherit the functionality? The answer is yes. Let's see how we can do that in the example in the following section.

Creating a base class

We create a `BaseView` class where common functionality such as the `render()` method is added. Then all other view classes can extend from this base class, and eventually inherit the rendering functionality. The following is the `BaseView` class with minimal rendering functionality:

```
// Parent view which has the render function
var BaseView = Backbone.View.extend({
  render: function () {
    var tpl = _.template(this.template),
      data = (this.model) ? this.model.toJSON() : {},
      html = tpl(data);

    this.$el.html(html);
    return this;
  }
});
```

Now, `UserItemView` will look much better. We will extend the `BaseView` class and will provide only the template as follows:

```
// A simpler view class
var UserItemView = BaseView.extend({
  template: '<span><%= name %></span>'
});
```

If you wish to add some extra functionality such as calling another function in your view's render() method, you can override the render method of the base class. Check the following example:

```
var UserItemView = BaseView.extend({
  tagName: 'div',
  template: '<span><%= name %></span>',
  render: function () {
    // Call the parent view's render function
    BaseView.prototype.render.apply(this, arguments);

    // Add your code here
    this.anotherFn();
    return this;
  },

  anotherFn: function () {}
});
```

There are a number of functionalities that you can move to your base class depending on your requirements. For example, in a non-trivial application, we often need to replace a view with another, destroy the old view by removing it from DOM, and clean up other dependencies. So, we can add a close() method to BaseView (as shown in the following code) that can take care of every view removal mechanism.

```
var BaseView = Backbone.View.extend({
  render: function () {
    var tpl = _.template(this.template),
      data = (this.model) ? this.model.toJSON() : {},
      html = tpl(data);

    this.$el.html(html);
    return this;
  },

  close: function () {
    // Extra stuff goes here

    // Remove the view
    this.remove();
  }
});
// This is not production-ready code, but it clearly gives you the
// concept of using custom widgets to reduce boilerplate in your code. It
// will not always be necessary to extend a Backbone class to create a
// plugin.
```

Developing plugins without extending base classes

Sometimes we find that creating a constructor function and adding methods to its prototype can be a better choice than extending the Backbone base classes. For example, in the `Pagination` plugin in the following code, instead of creating a `PaginationCollection` class by extending `Backbone.Collection`, we will prefer to go for a simpler class—a constructor function that accepts two arguments: a collection and the number of the items to be shown in a page.

```
// Pagination constructor function
var Pagination = function (collection, noOfItemsInPage) {
  if (!collection) {
    throw "No collection is passed";
  }
  this.currentPage = 1;
  this.noOfItemsInPage = noOfItemsInPage || 10;
  this.collection = collection;
}

// Use Underscore's extend method to add properties to your plugin
_.extend(Pagination.prototype, {
  nextPage: function () {},
  prevPage: function () {}
});

var User = Backbone.Model.extend({
  defaults: {
    name: 'John Doe'
  }
});

var Users = Backbone.Collection.extend({
  model: User
});

var paging1 = new Pagination(10, new Users());
var paging2 = new Pagination(20, new Users());
```

We didn't add the actual functionality, but just showed a skeleton of how the `Pagination` class may look. The benefit can be observed when you already have a collection and you want to implement pagination without extending a parent collection class. We added the member variables in constructor function so that individual instances of this class can have their own set of variables. On the other hand, the methods are added to the prototype of the class so that they are shared by all instances of the class.

This mechanism can be useful when you need a custom plugin that is not a type of Backbone view, model, or collection.

Understanding JavaScript mixins

In the previous section, we saw that inheriting properties from a parent class prototype provides a great deal of reusability. In some cases, we may want to re-use similar methods in multiple views, models, or collections. This can be achieved by creating a parent class that they can extend; however, it is not always a good practice as it creates some unnecessary layers and meaningless subtypes.

For example, assume that you want the view element of `UserItemView`, which already extends `BaseView`, to be draggable. So you include a `DraggableView` class that extends the `BaseView` class, and your `UserItemView` extends `DraggableView`. Now there is a sudden change in the requirement and you are asked to make the view named `UserItemView` a sortable view as well. Will you introduce another new class, `SortableView`, and put it somewhere in the chain? If yes, then this multitiered inheritance will surely create a logic that is absolutely unmanageable and frustrating. Look at the following figure that describes the situation in a better way:

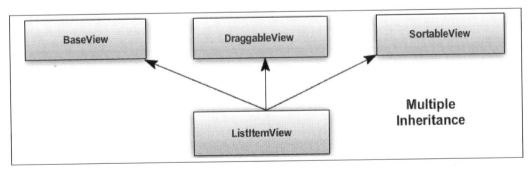

What is a mixin?

Fortunately, there is a feasible alternative in JavaScript, which is called **mixin**. In general computer science, a mixin is a class that provides a set of functions relating to a particular type. These mixin classes are not instantiated, but their functions are just copied to the main class to achieve a similar inheriting behavior without entering into the inheritance chain. Look at the following figure to understand the concept:

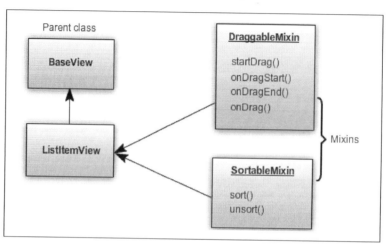

We have a `ListItemView` class that extends the `BaseView` class and represents an individual item of a list. Now we want these items to be draggable. How we can achieve this? How about adding a few methods in the `ListItemView` class that will take care of the dragging functionality? This approach will work, but what if we have few more components that need to be draggable too? Then we have to make a reusable object with these methods and use that object in all the required classes. This is what the mixin concept is—a collection of methods that will be copied to the class that wants this functionality.

Creating classic mixins

The most basic mixin definition will be a simple object with some properties such as the following code snippet:

```
// A simple object with some methods
var DraggableMixin = {
  startDrag: function () {
    // It will have the context of the main class
    console.log('Context = ', this);
  },
  onDrag: function () {}
```

```
}

// UserItemView already extends BaseView
var UserItemView = BaseView.extend({
  tagName: 'div',
  template: '<%= name %>'
});
```

We will use the Underscore method, `_.extend()`, to copy the mixin properties to the main class's prototype:

```
// We just copy the Mixin's properties into the View
_.extend(UserItemView.prototype, DraggableMixin, {
  otherFn: function () {}
});

var itemView = new UserItemView();

// Call the mixin's method
itemView.startDrag();
```

Note that the drag-related methods are now copied from `DraggableMixin` to its prototype. Similarly, we can use the same `_.extend()` method to copy the methods of `SortableMixin` to implement the sortable behavior without creating any multilayered inheritance.

Sometimes you may not want to copy all the methods of a mixin in your class. In that case, simply create a property in your class and copy the required function from the mixin in that property:

```
UserItemView.prototype.startDrag = DraggableMixin.startDrag;
```

This is helpful when you need only a part of the functionality from the mixin.

Creating functional mixins

There are some other ways of defining a mixin too. The following is an example of a functional pattern:

```
// Functional mixin
var DraggableMixin = function (config) {
  this.startDrag = function () {};
  this.onDrag = function () {};

  return this;
```

```
}

// DraggableMixin method is called passing the config object
DraggableMixin.call(UserItemView.prototype, {
  foo: 'bar'
});
// SortableMixin.call(UserItemView.prototype);

new UserItemView().startDrag();
```

The mixin here works as a verb, and this functional approach is well accepted in the community. The `this` function always refers to the receiver, that is, `UserItemView`. The functionality is exactly same but with a major difference—the `_.extend()` method is no longer needed and the mixin methods are not copied this time but are cloned instead. This is not a major problem—just the functions are redefined every time the mixin is used. However, this can also be minimized by caching the functions within the mixin. Let's see how we can achieve that in the next section.

Caching mixin functions

We can cache the initial function definitions by wrapping up the mixin in a closure:

```
// Functional mixin with cache
var DraggableMixin = (function () {
  var startDrag = function () {};
  var onDrag = function () {};

  return function (config) {
    this.startDrag = startDrag;
    this.onDrag = onDrag;

    return this;
  };
})();
```

The closure executes only once to define the methods even if the mixin is called several times. However, it raises another concern—inside the mixin methods, how are we going to use the `config` object that we are passing? This issue can be resolved by using an interesting pattern named `curry`.

Using curry to combine a function and arguments

As described by *Douglas Crockford* in his book *Javascript: The Good Parts*:

> *"Currying allows us to produce a new function by combining a function and an argument."*

Assume that you have a function and a set of arguments. You want these arguments to be combined with the function someway, so that when you will call that function without passing anything, the arguments will still be available to the function. See the following example:

```
// Simple function
function foo(){
   console.log(arguments);
}


// We want this bar object to be available in the foo() function
var bar = {
   name: 'Saswata Guha'
};

// Calling foo() without passing anything. Using curry, the
// function will have the bar object in its scope
foo();
```

The `curry()` pattern's definition is quite simple where this method is added to the function prototype, so when it is called on any function, it merges the arguments passed to itself with the arguments of the main function, as shown in the following code snippet:

```
// Definition of curry
Function.prototype.curry = function () {
   var slice = Array.prototype.slice,
      args = slice.apply(arguments),
      that = this;
   return function () {
      return that.apply(null, args.concat(slice.apply(arguments)));
   };
};
```

Now let's see how we can apply `curry` to our DraggableMixin function, so that the `config` object is available to all its methods, as shown in the following code snippet:

```
// Functional mixin with cache
var DraggableMixin = (function () {
  var startDrag = function (options) {
    console.log('Options = ', options);
  };
  var onDrag = function () {};

  return function (config) {
    this.startDrag = startDrag.curry(config);
    this.onDrag = onDrag;

    return this;
  };
})();


DraggableMixin.call(UserItemView.prototype, {
  foo: 'bar'
});
```

So, when we call `curry` on the `startDrag()` method, we pass the `config` object that we received while applying mixin, and it becomes available to `startDrag` as an argument. You can use either the classic or functional approaches for defining a mixin, though I personally prefer the latter.

Mixin is an important concept that many popular JavaScript libraries such as Sencha and Dojo follow. While the concept is quite easy, finding a proper context in an application to use a mixin is bit difficult. However, once you are aware of its use, you may soon find it beneficial to enforce reusability in your application.

Summary

If you ever checked the annotated source code (`http://backbonejs.org/docs/backbone.html`) of Backbone, you might have found that the library footprint is very small (the production file is only 6.4 KB at v1.1.0). Its sole purpose is to improve the structure and maintainability of your code with the least complexity. So, once you start using Backbone, you will find that in every step of the development, you need to write custom widgets and plugins. In this chapter, we learned the basics of Backbone.js and the utility of using Underscore.js with Backbone.js. We also saw how developing reusable components and custom pugins can reduce boilerplate from our code. In the end, we understood the concept of JavaScript plugins and discussed different approaches for defining mixins. We are going to use all these concepts several times in the following chapters.

In the next chapter, we will discuss different problems associated with Backbone views and possible solutions to them. We will also see how custom-view plugins or mixins can solve most of the problems.

2
Working with Views

Backbone view works as the presentation layer of an application. In simple terms, you can define it as an abstract layer for your HTML element. It doesn't contain any HTML markup of its own, but it contains the logic to present your model's data with the help of JavaScript templates.

If you go through the annotated source of Backbone view, you will find that `Backbone.View` is a small class with very few methods, including an empty `initialize()` method and an almost empty `render()` method, which are in general meant to be overridden by any custom view class. In this chapter, we will investigate some common problems and the solutions to these problems with respect to the Backbone views that developers face mostly while developing real-world Backbone.js applications.

The basic issues with Backbone are associated with view rendering or updating and maintaining multiple views within an application. We will analyze the following topics based on complexity:

- **Basic usage of views**: We will learn the basic concepts of Backbone view, its properties, functions, and event-handling.

- **Updating a view partially**: We will learn how to update only a part of a view without the need for re-rendering the complete view.

- **Nested views**: As the complexity of an application layout increases, we feel the need to maintain a hierarchy of multiple views. Nested views or subviews simplify event-handling and layout management to a great extent. We will explore the following topics:
    - When we need to use subviews
    - How to initialize and render nested views

- ○ How to avoid DOM reflow in the case of a large collection of nested views and a complex view DOM structure
- ○ How to clean up resources (child views, events) when you delete a parent view

- **Templates**: Templates are an essential part of Backbone and are used in combination with views to create reusable copies of HTML markup. We will discuss the following topics:
  - ○ The different options for storing and loading template files
  - ○ The advantages of template precompilation and storing precompiled templates on the client side
  - ○ The usage of template helper functions

- **Marionette views**: We can reduce the view boilerplate code using the custom view extensions of the Marionette library.

- **Layout manager**: We can simplify the complex layout architecture using the Backbone layout manager plugin.

Basic usage of views

Backbone views are the tools that provide a logical structure to the HTML markup of your application. Views represent the data of Backbone models or collections via JavaScript templates. For any change in the associated model or collection, you do not need to redraw the complete page, only update the relevant view—that's it. A basic view can be defined this way:

```
var UserView = Backbone.View.extend({
  render: function () {
    var html = "Backbone.js rocks!";
    this.$el.html(html);
    return this;
  }
});

// create an instance
var userView = new UserView();
$('#container').append(userView.render().el);
```

Here we created a simple HTML markup, placed it inside this view's element, and showed the view in the DOM. Let's understand the concept further by looking at all the steps.

Understanding the el property

What is the `this.$el` property? It is the property that points to the jQuery-wrapped version of `el`. Every view possesses an `el` property that either holds a DOM reference where the view is ultimately going to be rendered, or an HTML element that functions as the main element of the view. In the previous example, we didn't specify the `el` property. So, as soon as we instantiated the view, the `el` element was available to us though it was not rendered in the DOM. We had to do this rendering explicitly by appending the view element to the `#container` element. However, if we had mentioned the `el` property pointing to the `#container` element in the view definition or while creating it's instance, we wouldn't need to append it specifically to the document. Like the following code snippet:

```
var UserView = Backbone.View.extend({
  ...
  el: '#container'
});

// render it to document body
new UserView.render();
```

This generates the same result as the first example. However, this methodology creates problems when you make multiple instances of the `UserView` class, as all of them point to the same element as given in `el`, and because the last instance will overwrite the previous ones. However, this can be minimized if you pass the `el` property each time you create the view instance, though it is not a very good practice. Also, another problem related to view destroy still persists—if you destroy this view, it removes the `#container` element too—so, if you create another `UserView` instance passing the same `#container` element as the `el` property later, it throws an error. It is good practice to let the view create its own element and make the parent views or the layout manager take care of rendering the view.

There are some other properties that relate to the `el` property of the Backbone view; these are `tagName`, `id`, `className`, and `attributes`. The `tagName` property expects an HTML tag name as the value that the main element of the view will be created with. For example, if you specify `tagName` as `'ul'`, the `el` element that is created by Backbone will be an empty UL element. By default, `tagName` has the value `'div'`, that is, the view element will be a DIV element if nothing is specified as `tagName`.

The `id` and `className` properties specify the element's ID and CSS classes respectively. The `attributes` property holds all of the HTML attributes as an object:

```
var UserView = Backbone.View.extend({
    tagName : 'p',
    id : 'user_details',
    className : 'user-details',
```

```
        attributes : {
            'data-name' : 'User Details'
        }
    });
```

The resulting view element will look like this:

```
<p data-name="User Details" id="user_details" class="user-
details"></p>
```

Listening to view events

You can attach DOM event listeners to the DOM elements using the `events` property of view. These events can only be registered on the view element along with its child elements:

```
var UserView = Backbone.View.extend({
  html: '<button id="btn">Click me</button>',
  events: {
    'click #btn': 'onButtonClick'
  },

  render: function () {
    this.$el.html(this.html);
    return this;
  },

  onButtonClick: function () {
    console.log('Button clicked');
  }
});
```

We added a `click` event on the button and defined the handler to be called once the user clicks on that button.

Backbone delegates all of the view events, so that the events are attached even if the element is not rendered in the DOM. So, if you add one event hash for an element that is not yet available inside the view DOM, the event will be attached to it as soon as the element is rendered.

Displaying model data with templates

This is the most important part as the main purpose of a view is to display the data attached to it. In the simplest case, one Backbone view is attached to each model, and it keeps itself updated with the model change:

```
var User = Backbone.Model.extend({});

// UserView definition
var UserView = Backbone.View.extend({
// We will use Underscore template
  template: _.template('Hello <%= firstName %> <%=lastName %>!'),

  render: function () {
    if (!this.model) {
      throw "Model is not set for this view";
    }

    var html = this.template(this.model.toJSON());
    this.$el.html(html);
    return this;
  }
});

var userView = new UserView({
// Set a model for this view
  model: new User({
    firstName: 'Payel',
    lastName: 'Pal'
  })
});

$('#container').append(userView.render().el);
```

The preceding code is pretty simple to understand; here we pass a `model` instance to the view and set the model value to the template inside the `render()` function. Once rendered, the view will show the HTML markup with the model data.

We also need to ensure that the changes in any attribute of the model should be reflected in the view immediately. We can achieve this functionality by listening to the model's `change` event:

```
initialize: function () {
  this.listenTo(this.model, 'change', this.render);
  // Or, this.model.on('change', this.render, this);
}

...

// Change an attribute of the model
userView.model.set('lastName', 'Dey');
```

In the `initialize()` method, we listen to the model's `change` event and re-render the view. We can use both `on()` and `listenTo()` for this functionality, but the advantage of the latter over the former is that it automatically unbinds all the events that were added with the `listenTo()` method if the view is destroyed. On the other hand, you have to unbind these events explicitly if you bind events using the `on()` method.

In some cases, a model can have lots of attributes and you may not want to re-render the complete view every time an attribute changes. Rather, updating only that part of the view seems more practical. Let's see how we can partially update a view in detail in the following section.

Partially updating a view

Partial view updating is a common feature request that many developers ask for. The requirement is to re-render part of a view without rendering the complete view. This is pretty significant, mostly when there is a complex view with lots of data and only a small portion needs to be altered. Re-rendering the complete view for every small change can be a performance hit. The solution to this, on the other hand, is quite simple. In the following example, if the `address` attribute changes, then only the address part of the view's DOM will be updated, and the complete view will not be re-rendered:

```
...

template : _.template('<p><% name %></p><p><%= address %></p>'),

initialize: function() {
  this.listenTo(this.model, 'change:address', this.
showChangedAddress);
```

```
  },

  showChangedAddress: function () {
    // we are using the same main view template here though
    // another subtemplate for only the address part can
    // anyway be used here
    var html = this.template(this.model.toJSON()),

      // Selector of the element whose value needs to be updated
      addressElSelector = ".address",

      // Get only the element with "address" class
      addressElement = $(addressElSelector, html);

    // Replace only the contents of the .address element
    this.$(addressElSelector).replaceWith(addressElement);
  }

  ...
```

In this example, we populate the template with model data in the `render` function. Instead of listening to the `change` event of the model, we listen to the `change:address` event. Inside the `showChangedAddress()` method, we first create the HTML string with the template and latest model data. Then we extract the `address` DOM element from this HTML string. Finally, we just replace the view's present `address` DOM element with the latest one.

The same functionality can be achieved with a subview or child view as well, and this would be a better solution indeed. However, there can be situations when creating a new subview for such a small change is redundant and the previous solution might pay off. In the following section, we will understand the real scenarios in which (and how) we should use a subview.

Understanding nested views

A nested view or subview is basically a child view. The necessity of a subview arises when we have a complex view and we want to separate a part of it for the sake of simplicity, better event-handling, and a better model-view relationship.

To give you an example, assume that we have a collection of similar data and we need to display a list item for each type of data. In this case, it is always preferable to have separate views and models that give an option to control the behavior of the view attached to each model. When you click on an item, you may need to use the data for that item for further processing. If the item is a subview, we can get the data readily from the model attached to it. We will explain this concept in the example that follows.

We have seen `UserItemView` in *Chapter 1, Reducing Boilerplate with Plugin Development,* which uses the `User` model. Now, let's introduce a collection of user data that will be displayed as a list:

```
var User = Backbone.Model.extend();

// Users collection
var Users = Backbone.Collection.extend({
  model: User
});

// Add some data in the collection
var users = new Users([{
  id: 1,
  name: 'John Doe'
}, {
  id: 2,
  name: 'Dan Smith'
}]);
```

Initially, we will use only one view to render the complete collection by creating a `UsersView`:

```
var UsersView = Backbone.View.extend({
  tagName: 'ul',
  render: function () {
    var html = '';

    // Iterate over the collection and
    // add each name as a list item
    this.collection.each(function (model) {
      html += '<li>' + model.get('name') + '</li>';
    }, this);

    this.$el.html(html);
    return this;
  }
```

```
});

var usersView = new UsersView({
  // add the collection instance
  collection: users
});

// Display the view
$(document.body).append(usersView.render().el);
```

In the `render()` method, we iterate over all of the collection data and create an HTML list item that gets appended to an element of the `UsersView` class. This works perfectly and shows you a list of names.

The preceding implementation is absolutely fine, unless you want to receive a user's data by clicking on a user's name. In that case, we have to add the user ID somewhere in the HTML markup of the list item so that you can access it from the browser's event object:

```
html += '<li data-id="' + model.get('id') + '">' +
model.get('name') + '</li>';
```

On a `click` event, we call the `showUserName()` method that displays the name of the `user` model:

```
...
events: {
  'click li': 'showUserName'
},

showUserName: function (e) {
  var userId = $(e.target).attr('data-id'),
    user = this.collection.get(userId);

  if (!user) {
    return;
  }

  console.log('Clicked user\'s name =', user.get('name'));
}
...
```

The `data-id` attribute of the list element can be extracted from the `target` property of the `event` object and the model with the same `data-id` attribute can be obtained from `collection`. This methodology works fine unless there are lots of views in your application. Managing events in this way becomes tedious for large applications. So, how do we solve this problem? We use subviews!

Knowing when to use subviews

The previous pattern is similar to what we normally use in the case of simple jQuery-based applications where all of the data and events are tightly coupled to the DOM. Continuing event binding in this manner will ultimately result in much complexity at a later stage. A subview can simplify this process to a great extent. We will separate each list item and introduce a `UserItemView` variable for each of them:

```
var UserItemView = Backbone.View.extend({
  tagName: 'li',
  template: _.template( '<%= name %>'),
  events: {
    'click': 'showUserName'
  },
  render: function () {
    var html = this.template(this.model.toJSON());
    this.$el.html(html);
    return this;
  },

  showUserName: function () {
    console.log('Clicked user\'s name =', this.model.get('name'));
  }
});
```

It's simple. We just define one view for one model. In the `render()` method of `UsersView`, we eliminate the ugly HTML strings because we just need to create an instance of each subview (`UserItemView`) and append its elements to the main view:

```
render: function () {
  var userItemView;

  // clean up the view first
  this.$el.empty();

  // iterate over the collection and add each name as a list item
  this.collection.each(function (model) {
    userItemView = new UserItemView({
```

```
      model: model
   });

   this.$el.append(userItemView.render().el);
 }, this);

 return this;
}
```

We create new instances of `UserViewItem`, pass the model to it, and render it inside
the main view. The event listeners are now subview-specific and the subview methods
can directly access the model attached to it. This makes the application flow cleaner
and also eliminates the extra time that, though small, is required to look up the
collection for a particular model through its ID. If your view has multiple similar child
items, and each child item needs its own set of events, subviews are the right approach.

In the final section of this chapter, we will look at an awesome library, MarionetteJS,
which provides some useful readymade BackboneJS extensions. The `ItemView` and
`CollectionView` extensions provide a functionality that is similar to the previous
example but in a more robust and flexible way.

Avoiding multiple DOM reflow

We used jQuery's `$.append()` method to add the subview elements to the main
view. It is found that if there is a large collection of data, appending view elements
to the DOM one by one can create a severe performance issue; this will affect the
UI responsiveness of the application. The performance hit can be noticed even in
modern browsers, since every append causes a DOM reflow and forces the browser
to recalculate the size and position of the DOM tree.

This multiple DOM reflow can be avoided by using `DocumentFragment`, which is
described at `http://ejohn.org/blog/dom-documentfragments` by *John Resig* as *a
lightweight container that can hold DOM nodes*. We can collect all of the view elements
inside `DocumentFragment` and then append this fragment to the DOM. This will cause
a single reflow for the complete collection, and hence a performance improvement.

Let's see the `render()` method with a single reflow:

```
render: function () {
  // create a document fragment
  var fragment = document.createDocumentFragment();

  this.collection.each(function (model) {
    // add each view element to the document fragment
    fragment.appendChild(new UserItemView({
```

```
        model: model
    }).render().el);
}, this);

// append the fragment to the DOM
this.$el.html(fragment);
return this;
}
```

This process can enhance performance if there are many subviews and the view HTML structure is a complex one. In general, not many developers use it and you should go for it only when the HTML markup is a pretty complex one. For a simple HTML markup, the tests show almost no change in performance.

Re-rendering parent views

Imagine the following scenario where we need to show the company details along with a list of its employees. We will create two views here: a `Company` view that is the main view, and an `Employee` view that is a child view and represents each employee in the list:

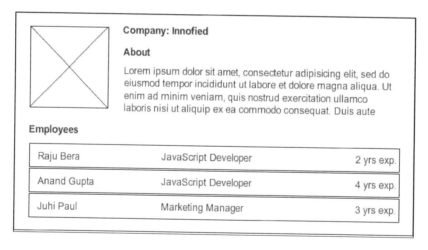

So, there will be a `Company` model and an `Employees` collection. We render the complete view along with the child views in a way similar to what we discussed earlier. If there is a change in the `Company` model, we will re-render the `Company` view, but that means we have to re-render all the child views too. Do we really need to do that? We actually do not need to, and we should not because that will be an overhead.

In most cases, as you re-render a parent view, it should not re-initialize its child views every time. So, it is preferable to initialize the child views in the `initialize()` method of the parent view, and add them in an array that can later be used in the `render()` method:

```
var ParentView = Backbone.View.extend({
  initialize: function () {
    this.subViews = [];

   // Initializing the child views
    this.subViews.push(new ChildView(), new ChildView()];
  },

  render: function () {
    this.$el.html(this.template);

  // Render each child view
    _(this.subViews).each(function (view) {
      this.$el.append(view.render().el);
    }, this);

    return this;
  }
});
```

This way, multiple calls to the parent `render()` method will maintain the state of the view and will only render the subviews again.

Removing parent views

In the previous scenario, where the company details and its employee list are shown, we assume a situation where we need to destroy this complete view and show a new view instead. Now, how do we destroy a view? We simply call the `remove()` method on it and it unbinds all the events that were registered with the `listenTo()` method. It also removes the complete view along with its child view elements from the DOM.

Are we unbinding the events of the child views here? No. The child views are removed from the DOM for sure, but we are not calling the `remove()` method on them. So, the models still exist and the events attached to the model still hold a reference to the view (or the view's methods). As a result, even if the view's `el` property is removed from the DOM, those view objects will not be garbage collected.

In order to prevent these memory leaks, we should always keep track of the child views while removing parent views. For instance, in the previous section we saw how we can store the child views inside a `this.subViews` array. We can override the `remove()` method in the `Company` view class and destroy the subviews individually before removing the main view:

```
var Company = Backbone.View.extend({
   ...
   remove: function () {
     _(this.subViews).each(function (view) {
       this.stopeListening(view);
       view.remove();
     }, this);

     Backbone.View.prototype.remove.call(this, arguments);
   }
});
```

This will ensure that all your child views are removed before the parent view. So, in order to get rid of memory leak issues, keep a few points in mind:

- Always have a reference to the current top level view
- Keep references of all the child views inside a parent view
- Ensure every event gets unbound

Also, if you are using any Backbone.js version older than V9.9.0, calling only the `remove()` method will not clean up the events, and you will have to unbind them explicitly. The same works for the events that you register using the `on()` method instead of the `listenTo()` method. For older versions of Backbone, you may need to use something like the following code:

```
remove: function () {
  this.unbind(); // Unbind all local event bindings

  // Unbind reference all such items
  this.model.unbind('change', this.render, this);

  // Remove this view
  Backbone.View.prototype.remove.call(this, arguments);

  // Delete the jQuery wrapped object variable
  delete this.$el;

  // Delete the variable reference to this node
  delete this.el;
}
```

There are a few tools that will help you check whether your application is leaking memory. You can track it with Chrome developer tools (`https://developers.google.com/chrome-developer-tools/docs/javascript-memory-profiling`), or you can use Backbone-Debugger (`https://github.com/Maluen/Backbone-Debugger`).

Working with templates

Templates are an integral part of Backbone application development. With Backbone, Underscore.js comes up with its inbuilt micro template engine, though we can use other popular template engines such as Handlebars, Mustache, or Jade too. In the following section, we will cover some interesting patterns with templates that will help you to manage the templates in large applications and enhance their performance.

Storing templates in an HTML file

In the simplest of cases, we store templates in two ways; we either directly add them inline within the view as a view property or add them inside the `script` tag in the `index.html` file. We have already seen the former case in the previous example. Let's see the second option:

```
<script type="text/template" id="tpl_user_details">
  <h3> <%= name %> </h3>
  <p><%= about %></p>
</script>
```

Here we just place the template string inside a `script` tag and give it a type `text/template` so that it doesn't get evaluated as JavaScript. You can always retrieve the template using the script ID:

```
var userDetailsTpl = $('#tpl_user_details').html();
```

 Default delimiters of the Underscore template are sometimes annoying and look ugly. A Mustache style {{}} looks cleaner and is preferred by most developers. You can easily transform your Underscore delimiters to the Mustache style with the `_.templateSettings` property:

```
_.templateSettings = {
  interpolate: /\{\{(.+?)\}\}/g
};
```

Both these cases of template storing work fine when the application is a small one. However, once the volume of the application starts to increase, it becomes quite difficult to manage the large chunks of template strings in the JavaScript file and the monster HTML file with all the templates of the application. There are a number of options to store the templates and use them. For example, we can create separate HTML files for our templates; this approach gives us benefits such as syntax highlighting, proper indentation, and options to manage the templates separately. However, this technique will lead to another severe issue—the templates will need to be loaded separately via AJAX requests. Such multiple XHR requests to load the templates in a large project is a bad idea and a huge performance hit; avoid it.

Let's look at some other options that may help you organize your templates in a better way.

Storing templates in a JavaScript file

Many developers suggest that though a template is a chunk of HTML markup, it's not completely HTML, and keeping the markup in a JavaScript file is a preferable option. We can create single or multiple .js files that include all the templates of the application. The templates will be stored in string format, but you can present them in a more human-readable way by using the join() method:

```
var TplManager = {
  templates: {}
};


TplManager.templates.userProfile = [
  '<h3> <%= name %> </h3>',
  '<img src="<%= avatar %> />"',
  '<p>Address : <%= address %></p>'
].join('\n');


TplManager.templates.userLogin = [
  '<ul>',
  '<li>Username: <input type="text" /></li>',
  '<li>Password: <input type="password" /></li>',
  '</ul>'
].join('\n');
```

You can maintain separate template files for your modules, for example, User.js and Dashboard.js. You can also have application-specific template namespaces, for instance, App.User and App.Dashboard. The crucial point is you can combine and minify these files later to get a single file that greatly improves the application performance.

For a large application, you may not want to store your templates in this way inside a JavaScript file, where you will not get any facility to format and highlight the HTML code. However, the usefulness of this pattern cannot be denied, more so when we get a single JavaScript file with a minified set of all the precompiled templates. In *Appendix B, Precompiling Templates on the Server Side*, we discuss this process in detail.

With the popularity of Require.js and **Asynchronous Module Definition (AMD)**, most developers today prefer storing individual templates in a separate template or in HTML files. Later, when the complete project's source code is optimized, it creates a single minified file with all the templates merged in JavaScript. This technique is now a popular approach, and we explained the functionality in detail in *Appendix C, Organizing Templates with AMD and Require.js*.

Precompiling templates

What is template compilation? In general, we create templates as strings and include template expressions in them. Once we pass that string for compilation, the template library analyze the string to create a format which can be applied with the data. This compiled function then returns another function where we pass the data and get the data integrated HTML string in return. This process is called template compilation.

Why do we need to precompile a template? This is because when we use a template string, say `TplManager.templates.userProfile`, multiple times, the same compilation process gets repeated every time. This is clearly extra work that will affect the performance of the app significantly. You can compare the difference in this jsperf test (`http://jsperf.com/underscore-templates-classic-vs-precompiled`) performed by Igor Hlina (`https://twitter.com/srigi`). The test shows that the precompilation of a template yields a 99 percent faster result than the classic approach.

By precompiling templates and caching them, you can reduce the overhead to a large extent. Let's add a method to our template manager that will compile a template only once and return the cached version every time:

```
var TplManager = {
  templates: {},
  cachedTemplates: {},

  // Returns compiled template
  getCachedTemplate: function (tplName) {
    // If compiled template already exists, return that
    if (this.cachedTemplates.hasOwnProperty(tplName)) {
```

```
            return this.cachedTemplates[tplName];
        }


        if (this.templates.hasOwnProperty(tplName)) {
            // Compile and store the template functions
            this.cachedTemplates[tplName] = _.template(this.
    templates[tplName]);
        }


        return this.cachedTemplates[tplName];
    }
};
TplManager.getCachedTemplate('userProfile');
```

So, we can access the compiled templates from the `getCachedTemplate` method. This is a non-optimized solution without much error handling, but the concept can be implemented for all your templates.

 The `_.template()` method accepts two arguments in general. If you pass both the template string and data, it will send you the complete HTML string with data. However, if you pass only the template string, it will return the function that takes the data as a parameter.

Avoiding evaluation in templates

I learned about many template best practices from the Sencha library. Sencha's `XTemplate` functionality doesn't let you add any JavaScript code evaluation inside the template string, but it provides a number of variables and options to add the custom functions that help keep the templates clean; I never found any issues while creating complex templates.

The Underscore.js template and most other template engines provide a functionality to evaluate the JavaScript code inside the template. On one hand, this looks pretty ugly, and on the other hand, it adds to the complexity as the number of templates increase in the project. Placing some JavaScript logic inside your template makes it very difficult to manage your code. So it is advisable to separate the JavaScript code from your HTML markup:

```
<h3>
  <%= companyName %>
</h3>
<ul>
  <% employees.forEach(function (employee) { %>
    <li>
```

```
        <%= employee.name %>
    </li>
  <% }); %>
</ul>
```

While displaying a list of employees, we need to iterate through the list and display the employee names. Underscore.js doesn't provide any inbuilt mechanism for this, but we can use a subtemplate here that excludes the evaluation part from this code. The subtemplate will be simple, such as this:

```
<li> <%= name %> </li>
```

You will iterate through the list in your JavaScript code, use this subtemplate to render only this `li` element, and then append the element to the main element. Though it might take a little more effort this way, it will help you avoid JavaScript evaluation in your template.

On the other hand, there are template engines such as HandleBars.js that provide inbuilt logic (for instance, looping, passing contexts, if-unless block helpers, and so on). So, if you feel that subtemplating involves more work, you can go for a better template library that may not be as lightweight as Underscore but provides more inbuilt helper functions.

Another idea to avoid evaluation in your template is to use helper functions. Let's take a look at them in the following section.

Using template helper functions

It is quite easy to use template helper functions. Imagine a situation where you are displaying a user's profile in your application. In the place of user's avatar, either you need to show a photo of the user or you must show a default avatar image. This is how you will write that condition in your template:

```
<% if(typeof(avatar) === 'undefined') %>
  <img src="<%= avatar %>" />
<% } else { %>
  <img src="images/default_avatar.png" />
<% } %>
```

This is an option, but we already decided not to evaluate JavaScript inside our templates. The helper function may come handy here. Try this function:

```
// A cleaner template
var tplString = '<img src="<%= getAvatar(avatar) %>" />';
var data = this.model.getJSON();
var html = _.template(tplString, _.extend(data, {
```

```
    // A template helper function to be merged with data
    getAvatar: function (avatar) {
      return avatar || "images/default_avatar.png";
    }
}));
```

So, while you are passing the data into the `_.template()` method, you need to make sure the template methods reside there as properties or subproperties. The question is why do we need to add the helper function as a part of the data? The reason is that most template libraries, including Underscore's template, create the data object that is passed to it the context of the function. So, the helper function is called on the context of data and can only be available in that way.

 There are a number of template engines that have some of the previous solutions inbuilt. If you are developing a small application, you may find Underscore's micro-templating solution enough for development. But if you are going to have complex templates in your application, we would recommend going for `Handlebars`, a popular and well accepted template engine.

Understanding automatic model-view data binding

Whenever an attribute of the attached model changes, we refresh the view to display the updated data. A `change` event listener is attached to the model inside the `initialize()` method of the view as follows:

```
this.listenTo(this.model, 'change', this.render);
```

However, there are options that can handle this data binding automatically and you do not need to take care of it for every model-view relationship. This principle is more aligned towards the MVVM design pattern than the Backbone's MV* pattern, and you will find it in frameworks such as `Knockout.js` and `Meteor.js`.

For Backbone, there are multiple plugins such as `Backbone.Stickit` (`http://nytimes.github.io/backbone.stickit/`), `Backbone.ModelBinder` (`https://github.com/theironcook/Backbone.ModelBinder`), and `Rivets.js` (`http://www.rivetsjs.com/`). These plugins provide a similar data binding feature. We are not going to discuss each plugin here; however, the implementation process is simple and similar for all of these plugins. If you wish to use such functionality, look into these plugins and use the one that fits your needs.

Using Marionette's ItemView, CollectionView, and CompositeView

Marionette (`http://marionettejs.com/`) is a composite application library for Backbone.js. Developed by Derick Bailey, it is a collection of common patterns and solutions to Backbone problems. It is a great library and lots of developers use it for their Backbone-based applications.

One important thing about Marionette is that it offers several separate packages for views, regions, and so on, and allows you to use any of them freely without requiring the complete library. In this section, we will explore Marionette's `ItemView`, the `CollectionView`, and the `CompositeView` functionalities. These views solve a number of problems we discussed in the previous sections.

ItemView

`ItemView` represents a single view for an item, it can be a model view or a collection view. It extends the `Marionette.View` class, which is a core view with a number of reusable functions. `Marionette.View` takes care of triggering, delegating, and undelegating events.

If you plan to use Marionette, views with a model or a collection should extend the `ItemView` class. It provides a number of functionalities including:

- A `serializeData()` method that is a generic method to return data for the model or collection that is attached to the view.

- A `close()` method that takes care of removing views from DOM and cleanup resources. This is similar to the `close()` method of the `BaseView` class we learned in *Chapter 1, Reducing Boilerplate with Plugin Development*.

- Some custom events such as:
  - The `'render'` / `onRender` event
  - The `'before:render'` / `onBeforerender` event
  - The `'close'` / `onClose` event
  - The `'before:close'` / `onBeforeClose` event

Let's look into a basic `ItemView` class definition as shown in the following code:

```
var UserItemView = Marionette.ItemView.extend({
  tagName: 'li',
  template: _.template('<%= firstName %> <%= lastName %>'),

  onRender: function () {
```

```
    // After render functionality here
  },

  onClose: function () {
    // Do some cleanup here
  }
});
```

We will create an instance of this and pass the model to it as follows:

```
var userItemView = new UserItemView({
  model: new Backbone.Model({
    firstName: 'Sudipta',
    lastName: 'Kundu'
  })
});


$(document.body).append(userItemView.render().el);

// Close and destroy the view after 2 seconds
setTimeout(function () {
  // userItemView.close();
}, 2000);
```

This is an example of a simple `ItemView` class, where we pass the model and use its methods to display the data. Have a look, we didn't provide any `render()` method definition here. It is because `ItemView` provides a simple rendering functionality by default. `ItemView` has a `serializeData()` method that sends the model data or the collection data attached to this view, and the `render()` method applies this data to its template and populates the view automatically with generated HTML content. Here is how the `serializeData()` method looks in Marionette:

```
// Serialize the model or collection for the view. If a model is
// found, '.toJSON()' is called. If a collection is found,
'// .toJSON()'is also called, but is used to populate an 'items'
// array in the resulting data. If both are found, defaults to
// the model. You can override the 'serializeData' method in your
// own view definition, to provide custom serialization for your
// view's data.
serializeData: function () {
  var data = {};

  if (this.model) {
    data = this.model.toJSON();
  } else if (this.collection) {
```

```
        data = {
          items: this.collection.toJSON()
        };
    }

    return data;
}
```

So, `ItemView` expects a template, a model, or a collection, and it reduces the initial boilerplate to render the view on its own. As you can see, a number of basic and reusable functionalities are handled in the `ItemView` class. It provides all the functions that we discussed in our `BaseView` class. Using it as a base class for your views can give a lot of flexibility while writing Backbone.js based applications.

CollectionView

A `CollectionView` class, as the name suggests, shows a list of items for each model item in the specified collection. The functionality is similar to the previous example, but much more robust with subviews. A `CollectionView` class creates an instance of `ItemView` for each data item and appends its elements to the main view's `el`.

Some of the common features of `CollectionView` are:

- Creating, adding, and removing child views.
- Displaying an empty view when the collection is empty.
- Automatic rendering and re-rendering for `'add'`, `'remove'`, and `'reset'` events of the collections, where the collection view automatically renders the changes.
- Provides a number of useful custom events:
    - The `'render'` / onRender event
    - The `'before:render'` / beforeRender event
    - The `'closed'` / `'collection:closed'` event
    - The `'before:item:added'` / `'after:item:added'` event
    - The `'item:removed'` event
    - The `'itemview:*'` event bubbling from child views
- Includes a `close()` method that removes the child views before closing.

Now let's use the previous `UserItemView` class as the child item and create a `CollectionView` class:

```
// Create a collection view and pass the item view class
var UsersView = Marionette.CollectionView.extend({
    tagName: 'ul',
    itemView: UserItemView
});

var usersView = new UsersView({
    collection: new Backbone.Collection([{
        firstName: 'Sandip',
        lastName: 'Maity'
    }, {
        firstName: 'Debopam',
        lastName: 'Biswas'
    }])
});

$(document.body).append(usersView.render().el);
```

Look how small the code is when compared to the code we developed earlier in this chapter to display a list of items. We just pass the class name `UserItemView` in the `CollectionView` instance as `itemView`, and it takes care of everything from rendering to destroying child items when the parent view gets removed.

Marionette's `CollectionView` reduces the boilerplate in your code to a great extent. If you are developing an application with multiple list type views, you can produce much cleaner code using Marionette's collection view, as it takes out most of the reusable functionality itself.

Working with CompositeView

A `CompositeView` extends from the `Marionette.CollectionView` class. In general, you can think of it as a combination of `ItemView` and `CollectionView`, where it accepts a model that represents a single dataset and a collection that displays multiple data. This is particularly useful when you have a hierarchical or a tree-like structure. You can relate it to the figure we mentioned in the *Re-rendering parent views* section. There we had to show data for the `Company` model and `Employees` collection together, and `CompositeView` would have been an excellent tool to provide a compact solution for that.

A composite view provides some specific functionalities apart from the basic
`CollectionView` functions, which can be explained as follows:

- Model data of `CompositeView` is applied to its template property.

- It has an `itemViewContainer` property that specifies within which element
  the collection view will be rendered. The `itemViewContainer` property
  should either be a jQuery selector or a jQuery object, or it can be a function
  that returns a jQuery selector or jQuery object.

- When `itemViewContainer` is not sufficient for specifying the exact position
  of `ItemView`, overriding the `appendHtml()` method of `CollectionView` may
  provide the desired result, as shown in the following code snippet:

```
appendHtml: function (galleryView, imageView, index) {
  // Put the imageView i.e. ItemView instances
  // inside element with class "box-result"
  galleryView.$(".box-result").append(imageView.el);
}
```

Let's assume a scenario where we want to display company details along with a
list of the employees. So, there will be a `Company` model, as shown in the following
code snippet:

```
// Company model
var Company = Backbone.Model.extend({
  defaults: {
    name: '',
    specialty: ''
  }
});
```

Similarly, there must be an `Employee` model for each employee too, as follows:

```
// Employee model
var Employee = Backbone.Model.extend({
  defaults: {
    name: ''
  }
});
```

Let's define an `Employees` collection for the employee list, as follows:

```
// Employees collection
var Employees = Backbone.Collection.extend({
  model: Employee
});
```

For the composite view, we want to present each employee as a separate `ItemView` instance so that event delegation becomes easy:

```
// Create an ItemView instance for the child items
var EmployeeItemView = Marionette.ItemView.extend({
  tagName: 'li',
  template: _.template('<%= name %>')
});
```

Now we can define the composite view that will display the model data and the collection data together, as shown in the following code:

```
// Create a collection view and pass the item view class
var CompanyView = Marionette.CompositeView.extend({
  template: _.template(['<h2><%= name %> </h2>',
    '<span><%= specialty %> </span>',
    '<ul class="employees"></ul>'
  ].join('')),
  itemView: EmployeeItemView,
  itemViewContainer: '.employees',

  // Add a company details to this view's model and collection
  addCompany: function (data) {
    if (!data) return;

    if (data.employees) {
      this.collection = new Employees(data.employees);
    }

    delete data.employees;
    this.model = new Company(data);
  }
});
```

Here, we first defined a template where we kept a place for the employee list to go. Then we mentioned the `itemView` option as the `EmployeeView` class that will be used by the collection to create an instance and populate it with each employee data. These item views will be stacked in the element mentioned in the `itemViewContainer` property. Now, let's create the composite view instance, add a company to it, and render it, as shown in the following code snippet:

```
var companyView = new CompanyView();

// Add a company details
companyView.addCompany({
  name: 'Innofied',
  specialty: 'Team of JavaScript specialists',
  employees: [{
    name: 'Swarnendu De'
  }, {
    name: 'Sandip Saha'
  }]
});

$(document.body).append(companyView.render().el);
```

The result we get is as shown in the following screenshot:

Innofied

Team of JavaScript specialists

* Swarnendu De
* Sandip Saha

So, you can see that a composite view provides a compact mechanism to display a model and a collection associated to it in a single view. You may have a tree structure data, and for that, multiple composite views need to be created. By default, the rendering mechanism of a composite view is hierarchical in nature and the `itemView` property is of the `CompositeView` type, if not overridden.

We hope we gave you a basic idea of all the Marionette views. Discussing all these views in an advanced level is beyond the scope of this book, but the Marionette docs will give you a complete description of the framework. We mention some resources and books about Marionette in *Appendix A, Books, Tutorials, and References.*

Using Layout Manager

When you work with multiple views in an application, it often becomes difficult to manage activities such as multiple view rendering, adding animation to an element, or replacing a view with another view. Let's look into a great extension, `LayoutManager` (`https://github.com/tbranyen/backbone.layoutmanager`), which provides a logical foundation to assemble layouts and views within the application.

Marionette too provides a similar functionality with its `RegionManager`, but we chose to discuss the `LayoutManager` plugin here because not everyone uses Marionette and this plugin can work independently with your Backbone app. If you are already using Marionette, I advise you to verify whether `RegionManager` solves your needs or not. Alternatively, you can use the `LayoutManager` plugin along with Marionette.

The `LayoutManager` extension provides solutions to a number of pain points such as:

- It handles asynchronous rendering of views if you are planning to dynamically load your templates from external files

- It defines the layout as an HTML structure and assigns the views to proper elements as given in the layout configuration

- It provides functionality to perform the following activities:
  - Insert views, apply data to the given template, and auto render them
  - Retrieve or remove views depending on multiple selection criteria
  - Cleans up views by unbinding all events from the view or from the model/collection that have this view as the context

We will look into these points by creating a simple layout as shown in the following screenshot:

There is a list of users, and when you click on a user item, the user's details are displayed on the right-hand side of the layout. You will find the complete code example with all HTML, CSS, and other files in our sample code. Here we will describe the parts that are critical.

We create a user model and collection first as shown in the following code snippet:

```
// Change template delimiter to Mustache type
_.templateSettings = {
  interpolate: /\{\{(.+?)\}\}/g
};

// User Model
var User = Backbone.Model.extend({
  defaults: {
    avatar: '',
    name: '',
    email: '',
    phone: '',
    twitter: ''
  }
});

// Users collection
var Users = Backbone.Collection.extend({
  model: User
});
```

We will have three views for this page: `UserList`, `UserItem`, and `UserDetails` views. The `UserItem` view will act as a subview of the `UserList` view. First, let's write the templates for these three views:

```
<!-- Layout manager template -->
<script type="text/template" id="tpl_main_content">
  <div id="main_content">
    <div class="user-list"></div>
    <div class="user-details"></div>
  </div>
</script>

<!-- User item template -->
<script type="text/template" id="tpl_user_item">
```

```
    <a class="name" href="#">{{name}}</a>
  </script>


  <!-- User details template -->
  <script type="text/template" id="tpl_user_details">
    <div class="avatar"><img src="{{avatar}}" /></div>
      <ul>
        <li><strong>Name:</strong>  {{name}}</li>
        <li><strong>Email:</strong>  {{email}}</li>
        <li><strong>Phone:</strong>  {{phone}}</li>
        <li><strong>Twitter:</strong>  {{twitter}}</li>
      </ul>
  </script>
```

The view templates are pretty simple. The layout template, which defines the structure of the page, is the most important here. The task has three aspects: you have to divide the layout in a number of sections as you want, add proper styles to align them, and then define your views inside the LayoutManager configuration that will automatically render the views inside these sections.

First, we will define the user list item that will display only the name of the user.

```
// UserItem sub view
var UserItem = Backbone.View.extend({
  tagName: 'li',
  template: '#tpl_user_item',
  manage: true,

  // LayoutManager uses serialize method to apply the data into
template
  serialize: function () {
    return this.model.toJSON();
  }
});
```

Notice the two new properties here: manage and serialize. The manage property is a Boolean property that determines whether a view will be treated as a layout or not. The manage property must be set to true if you intend to use the view inside the layout manager and handle its rendering function. You can also set it to true globally for all the views and specify it as FALSE if required for a particular view.

LayoutManager uses the serialize() method to apply the data to the view's template. The default implementation of the serialize() method returns an empty object. You should override it to send the data you want to display. Here we are sending the model data associated with the view.

LayoutManager provides two custom events, beforeRender and afterRender, to a view as it takes care of the render function itself. While using the beforeRender() method, the element of the view isn't yet available, but if you insert a view into the layout, LayoutManager keeps track of it and renders it once the parent view is available in DOM. We can use this method where we will iterate through the users' collection and insert the UserItem view to the list view:

```
// User List view
var UserList = Backbone.View.extend({
  tagName: 'ul',
  className: 'nav nav-tabs nav-stacked',
  manage: true,

  // Before rendering the list,
  //insert all the child list items into it
  beforeRender: function () {
    this.collection.each(function (model) {
      // insertview method inserts the views
      // directly inside the parent view
      this.insertView(new UserItem({
        model: model
      }));
    }, this);
  }
});
```

There are two similar methods insertView/insertViews and setView/setViews. Both these functions insert views into the layout according to the given selector name. The setView() method takes an extra insert parameter, which is a Boolean value, and determines whether the view will replace the complete content of the selector or will simply append to it. We create UserItem views, attach models to them, and insert them into the UserList view. The child views get automatically rendered inside.

We are done with the basic list definition. Now, let's define the layout manager functionality as follows:

```
// Create a collection with some data
var users = new Users([{
  name: 'John Doe',
  avatar: 'avatar.png',
  phone: '+88-888-8888',
  twitter: 'johndoe',
  email: 'johndoe@example.com'
}, {
```

```
      name: 'Swarnendu De',
      avatar: 'avatar.png',
      phone: '+99-999-9999',
      twitter: 'swarnendude',
      email: 'swarnendude@example.com'
   }]);


   // Define the main layout
   var MainLayout = Backbone.Layout.extend({
      template: "#tpl_main_content",

      // Assign the view to specific selectors
      views: {
         '.user-list': new UserList({
            collection: users
         })
      }
   });
```

The `LayoutManager` is also a type of `Backbone.View`, and you can render it as you do for any other Backbone view. In the `views` property, we can specify one or more view instances. In our case, we created the `UserList` instance, passed the collection to it, and let the `LayoutManager` take care of everything else to render it inside the `.user-list` element.

So, up to this point, we have our layout rendered with the user list inside. The only action remaining is to display the user details once we click a user item. Let's define the `UserDetails` view, which is a simple one:

```
   // User Details view
   var UserDetails = Backbone.View.extend({
      manage: true,
      template: '#tpl_user_details',

      serialize: function () {
         return this.model.toJSON();
      },

      // Set the selected model
      setModel: function (model) {
         if (model) {
            this.model = model;
         }

         return this;
      }
   });
```

This is exactly the same as our `UserItem` view definition with an extra `setModel()` method that sets the model to the selected one. Now we will insert this view into the layout when we click a list item. For that, we will add a click event handler to the `UserItem` view as shown in the following code:

```
var UserItem = Backbone.View.extend({
    ...
    events: {
      'click a': 'showDetails'
    },

    showDetails: function () {
      // Check Whether details view exists
      var detailsView = mainLayout.getView('.user-details');

      // If details view doesn't exist, create one,
      // set the new model and render it
      if (!detailsView) {
         mainLayout.setView('.user-details', new UserDetails().
setModel(this.model).render());
      } else {
         // Set the latest clicked model and re-render
         detailsView.setModel(this.model).render();
      }
    }
});
```

We use the `getView` method that can retrieve a view based on multiple criterion such as selector, model, or function. We check whether the details view is available or not. If not, we create a `DetailsView` instance, set the model, and render it. Otherwise, we reset the model and re-render the view.

So, we are done with the complete layout management. It is observed that most of the rendering functionalities are handled by the manager itself. This is just a basic example; `LayoutManager` can provide many more options and functionalities and eliminate 90 percent of your view management tasks. Do read their documentation thoroughly as you will be able to use most of it in your application.

Summary

In this chapter, we have gone through a number of important problems most Backbone developers come across, and learned multiple solutions to solve them. First, we discussed the partial view rendering and nested views. Any Backbone application needs to deal with nested views and if we can maintain their initialization, DOM reflow, and cleanup properly, it will greatly enhance the performance of the whole application.

We spoke about different template-handling methods, saw a number of solutions to load precompiled templates from external files, organized templates within applications, and understood how helper functions can eliminate evaluation of JavaScript codes inside templates and help us to create cleaner templates.

Finally, we learned about some of the very important extensions: Marionette's `ItemView`, `CollectionView`, `CompositeView`, and `LayoutManager`. All of these extensions provide great flexibility by taking out a lot of boilerplate code and managing your views by a great deal.

In the next chapter, we will talk about Backbone models; we will look into model data validation, different plugins for validation, model serialization, and the relational data model.

3

Working with Models

JavaScript models are an essential part of client-side data management. In stateful JavaScript applications, local or remote data is stored in models and the model provides a number of functions to work with this data such as conversions, validations, data persistence, and so on. Backbone models are no different than these and provide similar functionalities such as set/get data, validate, save to or fetch from the server, delete an attribute, and sync with the server.

In this chapter, we will discuss some basic problems with models that Backbone developers usually face, and will then propose some possible solutions to them. Also, we will cover a few interesting plugins and extensions for models that will help reduce boilerplate in your code. The main points to be covered are as follows:

- **Basic usage of models**: Learn the basics of Backbone models, such as important methods, properties, and data operations.

- **Validating the data**: We will see how basic data validations are done with Backbone models. Also, we will analyze an important plugin, `Backbone.Validation` that helps us reduce lots of boilerplate validation code.

- **Serializing models**: The data sent to the server or received from the server can be of different format than the format the model expects it to be. In this section, we will see how overriding the `parse()` and `toJSON()` methods help the model directly communicate with the server.

- **Understanding relational data model**: We will read an analysis of nested models and collections with the help of the Backbone relational plugin.

Basic usage of models

Models are one of the most important components of Backbone. Starting from storing data, they provide a lot of functionality, including logic around the data, validations, data interactions, and so on. A model can be defined by extending the `Backbone.Model` class, shown as follows:

```
var User = Backbone.Model.extend({});
```

A model consists of an `attributes` property that stores the data within it. You can get the model data using a `get()` method and set the data in `attributes` by using the `set()` method:

```
var newUser   =   new User({
    name : 'Jayanti De',
    age : 40
});


var name = newUser.get('name');   // Jayanti De
newUser.set('age', 42);


console.log(newUser.toJSON());
// Output => {"name": "Jayanti De", "age": 42}
```

The `toJSON()` method of a model returns a copy of the model attributes as a JSON object. Note that the output has `age` now set to the new value. Whenever you change any attribute via the `set()` method, a `change` event gets fired on the model:

```
newUser.on('change' , function(model, options){
    console.log(model.changed);   // Output => {"age" : 42}
});
```

The `change` event for each changed attribute also gets fired:

```
newUser.on('age:change' , function(model, newAge){
    console.log(newAge);   // Output => 42
});
```

This is quite beneficial when you want to update your views partially, because both the `change` and `change:age` events get fired in this case. You can listen only to a particular attribute change and act accordingly.

Using the defaults property

In some cases, you may want your model to have a set of default values until new data is added to it. Backbone provides a `defaults` property where you can specify the initial data, as shown in the following code snippet:

```
var User = Backbone.Model.extend({
  defaults: {
    name: 'John Doe',
    age: 20
  }
});

console.log(new User().get('name'));
// Output => John Doe
```

When added for every instance of the model, any unspecified attribute will automatically be set to the default value.

Avoiding object references in the defaults property

Make sure that you never use any object or array directly in the `defaults` property. This is because the objects are shared by reference in JavaScript, and if added into `defaults`, the objects will get shared among all the instances of the model. An example follows to explain the case:

```
var User = Backbone.Model.extend({
    defaults : {
        hobbies : []
    }
});

var user1 = new User(),
user2 = new User();

user1.get('hobbies').push('photography');
user2.get('hobbies').push('biking');

console.log(user1.get('hobbies'));
// Output => ["photography", "biking"]
```

You will see that the `hobbies` array now becomes a shared property between both the instances of the model. This is not a desired case and you should always avoid putting objects as default attributes. The solution to this problem can be achieved by using a function for the `defaults` property instead of an object:

```
defaults: function() {
  return {
    hobbies: []
  }
}

console.log(user1.get('hobbies'));
// Output => ["photography"]
```

This function will get executed every time a model instance is created, and thus will always send a new object for `defaults`.

Data interaction with the server

The Backbone model has made data operations with the server quite easy by providing a set of interesting methods such as `fetch()`, `save()`, `sync()`, and `destroy()`. Let's look into each of these methods one by one. We will use the same user model as we did earlier.

```
var User = Backbone.Model.extend({
  url: '/users'
});
```

Creating a model

In general, if you set new values to the model and call the `save()` method on it, your server should create a new model in the database. Next time onwards, the model will carry this `id` attribute and calling the `save()` method again should only update the model and not create a new one:

```
var user = new User({
  name : 'Ashim De',
  age : 55
});

user.save({
  success : function(){},
  error : function(){}
});
```

As no `id` attribute is present there yet, a POST request is sent to the `/users` URL and the server sends a response with the new ID.

Updating a model

Updating a model is also similar. If there is an `id` attribute present, the same `save()` method sends a PUT request to the server with new attributes:

```
var user = new User({
   id: 23,
   name: 'Shankha De',
   age: 14
});

// Send PUT request to the server
user.save();
```

Fetching a model

If the `id` attribute is present, the `fetch()` method of the model sends a GET request to retrieve and populate the model:

```
var user = new User({
   id: 23
});

// Sends GET request to /users/23
user.fetch();
```

Deleting a model

Use the `destroy()` method to delete a model. This method sends a DELETE request to the server with the model ID:

```
var user = new User({
   id: 23
});

user.destroy({
   success: function () {}
});
```

Validating the data

In Backbone, validation is taken care of by the `model.validate()` method. By default, the `Backbone.Model` class doesn't have a `validate()` method on its own. However, the developers are encouraged to add a `validate()` method that gets called by the model every time an attribute is saved or set with `validate: true` passed. A copy of the attributes is sent to the `validate()` method with all the changed values. Let's look at a simple data validation:

```
var User = Backbone.Model.extend({
  validation: {    emailRegEx: /^\s*[\w\-\+_]+(\.[\w\-
    \+_]+)*\@[\w\-\+_]+\.[\w\-\+_]+(\.[\w\-\+_]+)*\s*$/
},

  defaults: {
    name: '',
    email: ''
  },

  validate: function (attr) {
    if (attr.name.length === 0) {
      return 'Name is required';
    }

    if (attr.email.length === 0) {
      return 'Email is required';
    }

    if (!this.validation.emailRegEx.test(attr.email)) {
      return 'Please provide a valid email';
    }
  }
});

// Define the user view
var UserView = Backbone.View.extend({
  initialize: function () {
    this.model.on('invalid', this.handleError, this);
  },

  handleError: function (model, error, options) {
```

```
      alert(error);
    }
  });

  var user = new User();

  var userView = new UserView({
    model: user
  });

  // Set new attributes
  user.set({
    name: '',
    email: 'johndoe#www.com'
  }, {
    validate: true
  });
```

Here we created a model with the two attributes `name` and `email`, added a `validate()` method to test the values of these attributes, and defined a view that will handle the validation errors, if any.

As we are setting both the values in a single `set()` method, the `validate()` method will be called only once. However, it will return an error as soon as it finds an invalid attribute. What if we want to display all the errors together on our form? In that case, we must return an array or an object with all the error messages as shown in the following code snippet:

```
  validate: function (attr) {
    var errors = {};

    if (attr.name.length === 0) {
      errors['name'] = 'Name is required';
    }

    if (attr.email.length === 0) {
      errors['email'] = 'Email is required';
    }

    if (!this.validation.emailRegEx.test(attr.email)) {
      // If already there is an error for email,
      // then skip other errors for email
```

```
      errors['email'] = errors['email'] || 'Please provide a valid
email';
    }

  return errors;
}

// Set both empty values
user.set({
  name: '',
  email: 'johndoe#www.com'
}, { validate: true });
```

Now, we will receive an object with all the errors. This is useful while you need to show data individually even when they are set one by one. For example, this will be handy while we want to validate a field on blur event.

Using the Backbone.Validation plugin

So, we just saw a simple implementation of data validation. However, when there are lots of form fields with multiple validation criteria, the `validate()` method becomes too large with several nested if-else conditions. Creating the complete validation logic from scratch may make it more complicated and time-consuming. Fortunately, there is a wonderful plugin called `Backbone.Validation` (http://thedersen.com/projects/backbone-validation/), which makes things a lot easier by providing multiple built-in validation methods and simplifying the validation binding with views. Let's reimplement the previous validation with this plugin.

Configuring validation rules

There are a number of built-in validators, such as `required`, `maxLength`, `minLength`, `max`, `min`, `length`, and `pattern`. They are used as shown in the following code:

```
var User = Backbone.Model.extend({
  validation: {
    name: {
      required: true
    },

    email: {
```

```
        required: true,
        pattern: 'email'
      }
    },

  defaults: {
    name: '',
    email: ''
  }
});
```

There are some existing validation patterns such as e-mail, number, and URL. Alternatively, you can use a regular expression as a pattern. Similarly, you may need to define the complete validation functionality for an attribute rather than just a regular expression. In that case, you can add custom method validators to an attribute. Check the following example:

```
var User = Backbone.Model.extend({
  validation: {
    // Do not return anything if validation is passed
    name: function (value, attr, computedState) {
      if (!value) {
        return 'Name is required';
      }
    },

    // the method will be called on model's scope
    email: 'validateEmail'
  },

  validateEmail: function (value, attr, computedState) {
    if (!value) {
      return 'Email is required';
    }
  }
});
```

You can add the custom method to an attribute directly as a function or you can add the method name as a string, just like we did here. Every attribute can have one error message for each validation rule, or it can have a single one for all its validation rules. For example, in the following code, we provide separate messages for the `required` and `format` validations of `email`:

```
{
  name: {
    required: true,
    msg: 'Name is required'
  },

  email: [{
    required: true,
    msg: 'Email is required'
  }, {
    pattern: 'email',
    msg: 'Please provide a valid email'
  }]
}
```

Prevalidating a model with the preValidate() method

This plugin provides another important functionality to prevalidate an attribute of the model without touching the model itself, shown as follows:

```
var errorMessage = model.preValidate('attributeName', 'Value');
```

So, the attribute will be validated against the set of validators assigned to it, and the return value will be an error message if validation fails.

The `Backbone.Validation` plugin is very effective if your application needs several form validations. It removes a lot of boilerplate from your code base and provides a simple yet robust validation mechanism.

Serializing models

So far, the model data we used in our examples in the previous chapters are all simple data objects with attributes. However, there might be a case where the server is sending a different data format and you need to extract the essential part from it and apply it to the related model. For example, consider the following data:

```
{
  "name": "John Doe",
  "email": "johndoe@example.com"
}
```

Instead of sending the preceding data, the server returns the following data:

```
{
  "user": {
    "name": "John Doe",
    "email": "johndoe@example.com"
  }
}
```

This data cannot be applied directly to a model with the attributes `name` and `email`. If we call the `fetch()` method on the model now, it will just add another attribute named `user` to the model. The method that can help us overcome this issue is called `parse()`. By default, this method just passes the server response and the model applies whatever it receives from the `parse()` method. Here is how it is defined in `Backbone.js`:

```
parse: function (resp, options) {
  return resp;
}
```

However, we can override the `parse()` method to modify the raw server response and send back only the attribute `hash`. For this case, an object with the `name` and `email` attributes should be returned from the `parse()` method, as shown in the following code snippet:

```
var User = Backbone.Model.extend({
  url: 'server.json',
  defaults: {
    name: '',
    email: ''
  },

  // Returns the attribute hash
  parse: function (response) {
    return response.user;
  }
});

var user = new User();
user.fetch({
  success: function () {
    console.log(user.get('name')); // John Doe
  }
});
```

Here, the `server.json` file consists of the newly formatted data. In the `parse()` method, we are parsing the response and returning data that the Backbone model can accept.

 Remember that the `fetch()` method will not clear your model, but will extend the attributes only. So if in our case, the server sends only an e-mail in the response, the previous e-mail will get updated, but the name will still be what it was.

Similar to fetching data from the server, sending data to it can also face the same problem, that is, the server may expect the exact format in which it sends data to the model. Now, if we call the `save()` method on the model, it will send the data in the following format:

```
{
    name : 'Swarnendu De',
    email: 'swarnendu@email.com'
}
```

So, if the server expects the data in the same format as it is sending now, we need to override the `toJSON()` method, which is pretty straightforward. In the following code, we create a new object with the `user` property and return that object from the `toJSON()` method:

```
// Add this method to model
toJSON: function () {
  return {
    user: _.clone(this.attributes)
  }
}

// Let's set new data and send that to the server
user.set({
  name: 'Swarnendu',
  email: 'swarnendu@email.com'
});

user.save();
```

The request will be sent to the server with the following data, which is exactly what we were looking for:

```
{
  "user": {
    "name": "Swarnendu",
```

```
        "email": "swarnendu@email.com"
    }
}
```

However, this process has a downside. In most cases, we use the `toJSON()` method to get the model attributes hash directly. As we are overriding this method here, the data returned will differ from the expected data. So, you need to decide whether you will follow this approach to serialize the model or implement server-side interaction separately. If you go for this process, remember to apply the model data accordingly in your views when using the `toJSON()` method. Or alternatively, you can clone the `model.attributes` property to get the `hash` attribute:

```
var jsonData = _.clone(this.attributes);
```

 It is better not to use the `model.attributes` property directly. Manipulating the `hash` attribute directly can potentially cause some unexpected consequences, as the object will be passed by reference.

Understanding the relational data model

All the examples we have gone through so far have used simple models to represent data. However, in any nontrivial application, the data structure is much more complex, and the relationships among entities are multi-relational. For any medium- or large-level application, there will be lots of one-to-one, one-to-many, and many-to-one relations. Keeping these relations synced with the server often becomes a tedious job, especially while saving or fetching data with multiple requests.

While researching for this book, I found that most Backbone developers, at some point of their learning phase, have faced issues with nested models and collections. Fortunately, there is a great plugin known as Backbone-relational (`http://backbonerelational.org/`), developed by Paul Uithol, which minimizes the Backbone model hand-holding by syncing the model and all its related models with a single `save()` or `fetch()` method. It provides some great features that include the following:

- Bidirectional relations that notify related models of changes through events
- Control over how relations are serialized
- Automatic conversion of nested objects in a model's attributes into model instances
- Easy retrieval of a set of related models
- Determining the type of `HasMany` collections

We will look into a simple example with company-employee relationship to explain the concept of the Backbone-relational plugin:

```javascript
var Company = Backbone.RelationalModel.extend({
  defaults: {
    name: ''
  },
  relations: [{
    // 'type' can be HasOne or HasMany
    // or a direct reference to a relation
    type: Backbone.HasMany,

    // 'key' refer to an attribute name of the related model
    key: 'employees',
    relatedModel: 'Employee',

    // a collection of the related models
    collectionType: 'Employees',

    // defines the reverse relation with this model
    reverseRelation: {
      key: 'worksIn',
      includeInJSON: 'id'
      // 'relatedModel' is automatically set to 'Company';
      // the 'relationType' to 'HasOne'.
    }
  }]
});

var Employee = Backbone.RelationalModel.extend({
  defaults: {
    name: '',
    worksIn: null
  }
});

var Employees = Backbone.Collection.extend({
  model: Employee
});
```

Here we created a company-employees one-to-many relationship. In the company model configuration, you need to define the relation type that is used to create a `Backbone.Relation` instance at first. The `type` relation property can be `Backbone.HasMany`, `Backbone.HasOne`, or a direct reference to a particular relation instance. You also need to specify the attribute of the company model that holds all the employee models. Once the basic configuration is done, we will define the `Employee` model and `Employees` collection. Let's test the relationship with some dummy data now:

```
var innofied = new Company({
  name: 'Innofied'
});

var john = new Employee({
  name: 'John Doe',
  worksIn: innofied
});

var swarnendu = new Employee({
  name: 'Swarnendu De',
  worksIn: innofied
});

// 'employees' in 'innofied' now contains
// 'John Doe and Swarnendu De'
alert(innofied.get('employees').pluck('name'));
```

We've now created a fully-managed relation. When you add or remove models from `innofied.employees` or update `employee.worksIn`, the other side of the relation automatically gets updated.

The previous mentioned code is just an elementary example of the Backbone-relational model. Once you go through their complete documentation, you will find that the plugin provides many features that can enhance application development process to a great extent.

Summary

This chapter discussed some basic problems around Backbone models that lots of developers face, and described how we can approach these issues in our projects. We learned about basic data validation as well as getting all the error messages together from our validate method. Also, we saw how using the Backbone validation plugin can reduce our efforts when performing data validation by providing lots of inbuilt features.

If the data sent from the server has a different format from what a model expects, we now know how to override the `parse()` method to overcome this issue. Similarly, we override the `toJSON()` method to change the format of data that will be passed to the server.

For most nontrivial applications, a nested model relationship is an essential requirement, and the Backbone-relational plugin can provide a ready-made solution for that. The plugin is widely accepted by the Backbone community and a lot of projects are currently using it successfully.

There are some important topics to cover when working with models, such as collections, events, and sync. We are going to cover each of these points separately in the following chapters. The events and sync functionality is discussed in detail in *Chapter 6, Working with Events, Sync, and Storage*. In the next chapter, we will discuss the different functionalities of Backbone collections, basic and multiple sorting, filtering mechanisms, and collections with multiple model types.

4
Working with Collections

The purpose of the Backbone collection is pretty straightforward. As an ordered set of models, a collection provides a number of useful methods to play around with, including a set of Underscore.js utility methods. A collection includes functionality to add, remove, sort, and filter models, and save to or fetch data from the server. A collection listens to the events fired on its models–if an event is fired on a model of a collection, it will also be fired on the collection itself. This facility is quite significant when you want to listen to an attribute-change event of the model. We will look into it using some examples in the *Basic usage of collections* section of this chapter.

In the previous chapters, we saw a number of implementations of a simple collection to display multiple items in a list view. However, there can be cases where you want to sort the list with a number of criteria or you want to filter the list items to show only a particular type. In such cases, you have to either alter the collection to restructure the model positions or get the data that matches the filter condition. Let us look into what we will learn in this chapter:

- **Basic usage of collections**: Understanding the basic use of the Backbone collection and data operations with collections
- **Sorting collection**: Basic and multiple sorting of a collection
- **Filtering collection**: Performing basic filtering, avoiding re-filtering a filtered collection with duplicate collection, and filtering with full data pointers
- **Collection with multiple model types**: Managing a collection when a mixed set of data is passed from the server and each type belongs to separate models

Basic usage of collections

We will start looking into different features of the `Backbone` collection with a simple example. Let's assume we have a `User` model and a `Users` collection.

```
// Model definition
var User = Backbone.Model.extend({
  initialize: function () {
    this.on('change', function () {
      console.log('User model changed!');
    });
  }
});

// Collection definition
var Users = Backbone.Collection.extend({
  model: User,
  url : '/users',
  initialize: function () {
    this.on('change', function () {
      console.log('Users collection changed!');
    });
  }
});

var users = new Users(),
  newUser = new User({
    name: 'Jayashi De',
    age: 21
  });

users.add([newUser]);

// Change an attribute of the model
newUser.set('age', 22);
```

In the preceding code, simple model and collection definitions have been described. Here, we tried to demonstrate, as we mentioned in the introduction of this chapter, that any event fired on a model will get fired on the collection too. When you run this code, the model-change handler is run first, then followed by the collection change-event handler.

The `Backbone` collection provides a huge set of methods along with a number of `Underscore` utility methods to work on it. Because a collection deals with multiple data, you will find the `Underscore` utility methods are very useful to operate on it. Discussing all these methods and their functionality is beyond the scope of this book, but we are going to see how to use the `fetch()` and `save()` methods to retrieve data from and save data to the server using an AJAX request in the next section.

Performing data operations with collections

You can use AJAX requests to save and fetch data to and from the server. The result then needs to be applied on the collection. However, Backbone simplifies the complete process by providing a few methods such as `fetch()` and `save()` to directly interact with the server. We will use the same collection that we used in the previous section to demonstrate how we can perform all data operations with collections.

Fetching data from the server

Fetching data from the server is quite easy. You just call the `fetch()` method on the collection as shown in the following code line, and a GET request is sent to the URL that we added in the collection's configuration. It receives a JSON array with objects that get added to the collection as models.

```
users.fetch();
```

On receiving the data, the `set()` method of the collection is automatically called to update the collection. If a model doesn't exist, it gets added; if the model exists already, the latest data gets merged with it; and if the collection has a model that is not there in the new data, it gets removed.

Saving data to the server

Unlike fetching data from the server, collections do not have a method to store data as a whole to the server. Instead, the `save()` method of each individual model needs to be called as shown in the following code snippet:

```
var user = users.get(1);
user.save();
```

The `save()` method appends the model's ID to the server's URL (`/users/1`) and sends a PUT request to that URL. So, to save the complete collection to the server, you need to iterate through the collection and call the `save()` method on each model individually.

Sorting a collection

Sorting a collection is fairly easy with Backbone as built-in methods are already available for this purpose. To sort a collection, add a `comparator` to the collection, which in general, is a function that can take a single model or two consecutive models for comparison, or it can be a string that points to an attribute of its model. Whenever a model is added to the collection, the comparator sorts the collection accordingly. Changing an attribute of a model later doesn't initiate the sort functionality automatically and you need to call the `sort()` method on the collection again to re-sort it. Let's look into a simple example of sorting a collection:

```
var User = Backbone.Model.extend();

var Users = Backbone.Collection.extend({
  model: User,
  comparator: 'age'
});

var users = new Users();
users.add([{
  name: 'John Doe',
  age: 29
}, {
  name: 'Richard Smith',
  age: 35
}, {
  name: 'Swarnendu De',
  age: 29
}, {
  name: 'Emily Johnson',
  age: 25
}, {
  name: 'Sarah Castle',
  age: 40
}, {
  name: 'Ben Cooper',
  age: 29
}]);

console.log(users.pluck('name')); // ["Emily Johnson", "John Doe", //
"Swarnendu De", "Ben Cooper", "Richard Smith", "Sarah Castle"]

console.log(users.pluck('age')); // 25, 29, 29, 29, 35, 40
```

As you can see, the output is a collection sorted by age. Similarly, we can implement the alphabetical order with `name` as the comparator. The preceding functionality can also be replicated by the following two options:

```
// Underscore's sortBy() comparator
comparator: function (model) {
  return model.get('age');
}


// Underscore's sort() comparator
comparator: function (model1, model2) {
  return model1.get('age') < model2.get('age');
}
```

The first case is simple; it provides a string attribute to the comparator. The second case provides a comparison between two models (`model1` and `model2`). If the `age` attribute of `model1` is greater than that of `model2`, `model1` and `model2` will interchange their positions to be in ascending order.

Sorting a collection with multiple attributes

Note that there are three 29-years-old values in the example mentioned in the preceding section. What if we want to sort these models according to the `name` attribute too? The string comparison can also be done the same way as we did for numbers; the functionality will be simple (see the following example):

```
comparator: function (model1, model2) {
  // If age is same, then sort by name
  if (model1.get('age') === model2.get('age')) {
    return model1.get('name') > model2.get('name');
  } else {
    return model1.get('age') > model2.get('age');
  }
}

console.log(users.pluck('name'));
console.log(users.pluck('age'));
```

The preceding code only sorts the collection by the `name` attribute. If two models have the same age values, the result will look like the following:

```
["Emily Johnson", "Ben Cooper", "John Doe", "Swarnendu De", "Richard
Smith", "Sarah Castle"]
[25, 29, 29, 29, 35, 40]
```

A `sort` event is always fired when there is a comparator present in the collection and you add some data to it. It also gets fired when you specifically call the `sort()` method on the collection.

Filtering a collection

Filtering a collection is a fairly simple concept; here we want to get a part of the data based on a certain criteria. For example, if you have a list of items and you want to filter the list to only show a subset of all the items, you filter the attached collection. By default, Backbone provides some built-in functions that take care of basic filtering. The two methods `where()` and `findWhere()` produce similar functionality, though `findWhere()` only returns the first model that matches the condition.

Performing basic filtering

The `where()` method accepts a set of model attributes and returns an array of the matched models.

```
var users = new Backbone.Collection([
  { name: 'John', company: 'A' },
  { name: 'Bill', company: 'B' },
  { name: 'Rick', company: 'A' }
]);

users.where({
  company: 'A'
});
```

The result will be an array of two models that have A as their company. However, note that filtering the collection does not change the original collection data at all; instead, it just returns an array with the results. If there is a Backbone view that is displaying the collection data as a list, filtering the collection will not have any effect on the list.

So, how are we going to resolve this? One simple task can be done—let's reset the collection with the filtered data and re-render the list. The following code will work fine and the collection will only have the filtered data with it:

```
var filteredData = users.where({
  company: 'A'
});

// Reset the collection with array with filtered data
```

```
users.reset(filteredData);

// A collection with only filtered data
console.log(users);
```

Now, if you re-render the list, it will only show the filtered data. This looks fine; however, if you want to re-filter the collection, it will not be applied on the complete collection of data but on the previously filtered data. This is wrong; it is advisable to avoid such patterns that may lead to severe problems in a later stage. When you filter a collection only once, there should not be any problem, but multiple filtering of the collection will surely cause problems if the same collection is used elsewhere too. The following code, for example, will return zero results for the same reason:

```
users.where({
  company: 'B'
});
```

Let's attempt a few options to find a solution to this problem. We will first try this using a duplicate collection.

Filtering a collection with a duplicate collection

There are multiple solutions to the problem we found in the preceding section. For example, we can create another collection instance whenever a collection is filtered and we always reset this second collection with the filtered data. That way, the main collection will not be altered and passing the second collection to the view instance will produce the desired result.

```
var filteredData = users.where({
  company: 'A'
});

// Create a new collection that will only hold filtered data
var filteredCollection = new Backbone.Collection();

// Reset this collection every time
// there is a new set of filtered data
filteredCollection.reset(filteredData);

console.log(filteredCollection, users);
```

This time, the original collection holds its state and the new filtered collection provides the necessary functionality. This process can become quite beneficial for displaying a filtered set of data. The main disadvantage of this process is that you need to create another new instance of the collection in order to filter it.

Self-filtering with full data pointers

The disadvantage of multiple filtering can also be eliminated by keeping a reference to the complete dataset before applying filters. If we can save the initial data in a property inside the collection itself and then apply a filter on it, the collection data gets changed but the raw data is still available. Therefore, if we need to re-apply another filter on the collection, we can first reset it with the total data and then apply the new filter. To understand the concept with an example, we will define a custom `FilterCollection` class:

```
var FilterCollection = Backbone.Collection.extend({
  _totalData: [],
  _isFiltered: false,

  initialize: function (data) {
    // The initial data sent to collection will be saved
    if (data) {
      this._setTotalData(data);
    }

    // If some data is added later,
    // that should reflect in _totalData
    this.on('add', function () {
      this._setTotalData();
    }, this);
  },

  // Every time a new data has been added to the collection
  _setTotalData: function (data) {
    this._totalData = data || this.toJSON();
  },

  // Apply a new filter to the collection
  applyFilter: function (criteria) {
    // Clear the previous filter
    this.clearFilter();

    // Apply new filter
```

```
        this.reset(this.where(criteria));

        // Mark this as filtered
        this._isFiltered = true;
    },

    // Clear all filters applied to this collection
    clearFilter: function () {
        // skip first reset event while the collection
        // has the original data
        if (this._isFiltered) {
            // Reset the collection with complete data set
            this.reset(this._totalData);
            this._isFiltered = false;
        }
    }
});
```

We create a custom `Collection` class that has a `_totalData` property, which is supposed to hold the complete data of that collection. In the `initialize` method, we check whether any data has been passed to the collection; if it has been passed, we save that data in this variable. We also include an `add` event listener so that the newly added data gets reflected.

Now, once you call the `applyFilter()` method on the collection, it first resets the collection with full data and then applies the filter on this collection. That way, each time you filter the collection with this method, you do not need to worry about whether it is being applied to the previously filtered collection or not. Let's analyze the functionality with a test case:

```
var filteredCollection = new FilterCollection ([
    { name: 'John', company: 'A' },
    { name: 'Bill', company: 'B' },
    { name: 'Rick', company: 'A' }
]);

// Add another data to check whether add event is working or not
filteredCollection.add({
    name: 'John',
    company: 'C'
});

// Filter with company
filteredCollection.applyFilter({
    company: 'A'
```

```
});

// Filter with name
filteredCollection.applyFilter({
  name: 'John'
});

console.log(filteredCollection);
// Shows two data both with name : 'John'
```

Earlier, after second-time filtering, you received only one set of data because the collection had been filtered twice and the returned model had the name John and the company A. But now, because the collection is refreshed before every filtering, you will get a proper result.

The preceding code is not ready for production, and you need to make it more sophisticated so that _totalData should always have the latest data. Anyhow, the pattern comes useful in certain cases, and keeping a filterable collection extension or a Filterable mixin ready can get you an immediate solution.

Understanding the collection of multiple model types

There are cases when we have a mixed set of data coming from the server and we need to put the complete data in a single collection. For example, assume that the server is sending the complete employee details of a company. Now, there are different types of employees—developers, managers, designers, and so on, and you want to have different model types for each of these. How is the collection supposed to hold all types of models together? Here is an example with which you can get the desired functionality:

```
var Employee = Backbone.Model.extend();
var Developer = Employee.extend();
var Manager = Employee.extend();

var Employees = Backbone.Collection.extend({
  url: 'employees.json',
  model: function (attrs, options) {
    // For each data, check the attribute type
    switch (attrs.type) {
      case "Developer":
        return new Developer(attrs, options);
```

```
        break;

    case "Manager":
        return new Manager(attrs, options);
        break;
    }
  }
});

var employees = new Employees();
employees.fetch();
console.log(employees);
```

The model that a collection asks for is either the model itself, an instance of it that is created every time data is added to the collection, or can hold a function to which data attributes are passed to and you can check for the related model according to the data and pass an instance of it. Here, in the preceding example, we did the same thing and returned separate models depending on the type of data attribute.

Summary

Working with collections is a basic requirement of Backbone, and the questions associated with a collection are related to the models too. For example, the most common issue that almost every developer faces is nested collections, and the solution to the problem is related to how the data is parsed inside the model itself. We discussed the relational data plugin in *Chapter 3, Working with Models*, that wonderfully solves the problem with nested models and collections. It is highly recommended to use this plugin for any such data relationships.

This chapter discussed how we can sort and filter collections. Simple sorting and multiple sorting processes were described with examples. We also saw a number of methods for filtering a collection, which can be useful in different situations.

A collection can hold different types of model data inside—the solution to which was described with an example. In general, any dataset needs a handful of utility methods to work with. A large set of Underscore.js utility methods made it much easier for us to work with Backbone collections.

In the next chapter, we are going to discuss the necessities of Backbone routers and why the use of multiple subrouters is beneficial for uncomplex applications.

5
Routing Best Practices and Subrouting

A router is one of the most useful objects in Backbone; it is mainly used to route application URLs using hash fragments or standard URLs. In the earlier versions of Backbone, `Backbone.Controller` was used to take care of routing as well as default controller tasks, instead of `Backbone.Router`. Later, it was changed to `Backbone.Router`, because the router is meant to only handle routing client side pages and connect them to events and actions via URLs, while the functional logic must be taken care of by the presenters (that is, Backbone views). The concept of a router is pretty straightforward—it matches the method name to the URL fragment and calls the method. The method then takes care of the events and actions as required.

In this chapter, we will learn about some best practices, such as how to organize routers for medium- and large-scale applications, and which types of tasks should be handled by a router. The main topics to be covered are as follows:

- **Working with routers**: This provides a basic example of how routers work, along with an analysis of what can go wrong while working with routers.

- **Best practices for working with routers**: We will look into some good practices that one should follow while working with routers.

- **Subrouting – a key to organize complex apps**: Once your application grows, maintaining a single router becomes a mammoth task. Dividing the app router into multiple subrouters is a preferable way to manage it.

Working with routers

The Backbone router provides methods to route client-side pages by using hash fragments or standard URLs as per the History API. Routes that use the hash fragments or History API may look like this:

```
// Hash fragment
http://www.foo.com/#user/23

// Standard URL
http://www.foo.com/user/23
```

The routes and actions that will be triggered when the URL fragment matches the specific routes are defined in the routes object of the router:

```
routes: {
  'users' : 'showUsers',
  'user/:id' : 'showUserDetails',
  'user/:id/update' : 'updateUser'
}
```

Now, let's see how we can create a basic router. Assume that we are developing an application with a few modules, among which the User module is an important one.

```
var AppRouter = Backbone.Router.extend({
  routes: {
    'users': 'showUsers',
    'user/:id': 'showUserDetails',
    'user/:id/update': 'updateUser',
    'user/:id/remove': 'removeUser'
  },

  showUsers: function () {
    // Get all the user details from server and
    // show the users view
  },

  showUserDetails: function (userId) {
    // Get the user details for the user id as received
  },

  updateUser: function (userId) {},
  removeUser: function (userId) {}
});
```

Quite simple! There are a number of options that modify the routes to get the expected result. For example, you can use "splats" or optional parts in a route; for a detailed overview of routes, refer to the Backbone.js API at `http://backbonejs.org/#Router`.

In the preceding example, all the show methods (`showUsers()` and `showUserDetails()`) will most likely create the view instances, send AJAX requests to the server to get their details, and then show the views in the DOM. Similarly, the update and delete methods will also send requests to the server for the desired actions to be taken. Now, assume the `User` module has multiple other methods in this router along with these CRUD methods. In addition, the entire application has a number of similar modules whose routes will also get added to this router. As a result, the router will soon become a gigantic one with hundreds of lines of code; this is something that is beyond our control.

We should take care of a few things while working with routers and avoid such situations. We will look at some good practices in the following section that will make our routers simple, flexible, and easy-to-maintain.

Best practices for working with routers

Working with a Backbone router is fairly easy when the application is of a small size. However, as the complexity increases, maintaining a router becomes difficult unless some rules are followed. In the following section, we will discuss some points that you should take care of while using routers.

Avoiding large functional code in route methods

Though the basic task of a router is to monitor the routes and trigger functions, it manages some business logics of the app too. In an MVC architecture, the task of a controller is to handle the data request that is sent from the client and work upon the data that comes from the server in response. Similarly for a router, since the URL fragments reflect some part of the application's data, the data communication, calling view methods, or updating model attributes are done using router methods.

A trend I often see in beginner-level developer code is that they frequently include a large chunk of functional code inside the router methods. On one hand, this increases the size of the router, and on the other hand, it complicates the logic. It is always advisable to keep your router methods as short as possible by pushing the functional logic in views and using events instead of callbacks. In the following section we will see how we can keep our router clean. Also, we will look at event delegation, custom events, and callback methods in more detail in *Chapter 6, Working with Events, Storage, and Sync*.

Instantiating views in router methods

I have seen many developers who instantiate their application views inside router methods. While there is no such restriction in instantiating views or modifying DOM elements in router methods, it is a good practice to avoid such operations in routers. This is somewhat related to the first point that I mentioned in this section. In the following code, we have instantiated a `UserView` class and rendered it in the DOM inside the router method:

```
Backbone.Router.extend({
  routes: {
    "users": "showUsers"
  },

  showUsers: function () {
    var usersView = new UsersView();
    usersView.render();
    $("#user_list").html(usersView.el);
  }
});
```

This looks simple and works perfectly. But will it not clutter the router if there are 20 or more such methods? Why not create a controller or a high-level application object and add the method there? Then you can call this controller method from the router method as follows:

```
Backbone.Router.extend({
  routes: {
    "users": "showUsers"
  },

  showUsers: function() {
    UserController.showUsers();
  }
});

var UserController = {
  showUsers: function() {
    var usersView = new UsersView();
    usersView.render();
    $("#user_list").html(usersView.el);
  }
}
```

Now any change in the `showUsers()` method functionality will not force you to touch the router. There's really not much of a visible difference—but personally, as I have used the second pattern several times and benefited from it, I can guarantee you that the separation of concern will produce a much cleaner router along with a maintainable code base.

Also, in this context, we recommend you check out `Marionette.AppRouter` (`https://github.com/marionettejs/backbone.marionette/blob/master/docs/marionette.approuter.md`) and `Marionette.Controller` (`https://github.com/marionettejs/backbone.marionette/blob/master/docs/marionette.controller.md`). Marionette `AppRouter` and `Controller` work in the same way as our `UserController` and the base router. The controller actually does the work (such as assembling the data, instantiating the view, displaying them in regions) and can update the URL to reflect the application's state (for example, displayed content). The router simply triggers the controller action based on the URL that has been entered in the address bar. Both these classes are quite useful, and you can go for either of them if needed.

Using regular expressions for selective routing

If you want to trigger a router method only when a specific condition is matched, a **regular expression** comes to the rescue. Regular expressions are flexible with routes and Backbone supports them completely. In fact, all of the routes are first converted into `RegExp` objects when they are added to the routing table.

However, JavaScript will not allow you to add a regular expression as a property of the `routes` object, unlike the other string URL fragments:

```
// This will give error
routes : {
  /^user\/(\d+)/ : 'showUserDetails'
}
```

The solution is that you can add the regular expression in the `routes` object in the `initialize()` method of the router:

```
initialize: function () {
  this.route(/^user\/(\d+)/, 'showUserDetails');
},

showUserDetails: function (id) {
  console.log(id);
}
```

This is an example where only numbers are allowed in the URL fragment after #user. If you try to open a URL ending with #user/abc, the showUserDetails() method will not be called, but with the URL fragment #user/123, the same method will be triggered. So, this is a very generic example of using a regular expression as a route. Regular expressions are very useful for more complex levels of URL fragments in order to provide a level of restriction.

Subrouting – a key to organizing complex apps

Subrouting is the idea of dividing an application's router into a number of module-specific routers. In a small- or medium-level application, you may never need something like this. However, for an application with multiple modules, a single router that handles all of the routes soon turns into a huge, unmanageable class. So, it is always preferable to split the main router into a set of module-specific routers.

Backbone.Subroute (https://github.com/ModelN/backbone.subroute), a wonderful extension developed by Dave Cadwallader, provides the functionality that we are talking about. It lets the base router delegate all of the module-specific routes to the subrouter associated with that module. Let's understand the difference between a router and subrouter with the two examples that follow.

The all-in-one router

The following is the code for a single router that handles the routes of all the modules of an application:

```
var App = {};

var App.BaseRouter = Backbone.Router.extend({
  routes: {
    // Generic routes
    '': 'showHome',
    'logout': 'doLogout',

    // User specific routes
    'users/view/:id': 'showUserDetails',
    'users/search': 'searchUsers',

    // Company specific routes
```

```
    'company/:id': 'showCompanyDetails',
    'company/users': 'showCompanyDetails'
  },

  showHome: function () {},
  doLogout: function () {},

  showUserDetails: function () {},
  searchUsers: function () {},

  showCompanyDetails: function () {},
  showCompanyDetails: function () {},
});
```

Now, let's use `Backbone.Subroute` and see how to define the base router and module-specific routers. With `Subroute`, the base router becomes a tiny router that only takes care of the router redirections.

The base router

The following is the code for the base router:

```
var App.BaseRouter = Backbone.Router.extend({
  routes: {
    // Generic routes
    '': 'showHome',
    'logout': 'doLogout',

    // Route all users related routes to users subroute
    'users/*subroute': 'redirectToUsersModule',

    // Route all company related routes to company subroute
    'company/*subroute': 'redirectToCompanyModule'
  },

  showHome: function () {},
  doLogout: function () {},

  redirectToUsersModule: function () {
    if (!App.usersRouter) {
      App.usersRouter = new App.UsersRouter('/users');
    }
  },

  redirectToCompanyModule: function () {
```

```
      if (!App.companyRouter) {
        App.companyRouter = new App.CompanyRouter('/company');
      }
    },
  });
```

The Users module router

The following is the code for the `Users` module router:

```
var App.UsersRouter = Backbone.SubRoute.extend({
  routes: {
    '': 'showUsers',
    'view/:id': 'showUserDetails',
    'search': 'searchUsers'
  },

  showUsers: function () {},
  showUserDetails: function () {},
  searchUsers: function () {}
});
```

Look at the base router. What we are doing here is pretty simple—we use a wildcard (or splat) to trigger a method that lazily instantiates a subrouter and passes the initial parameter of the hash. Now, because `Backbone.Subroute` extends Backbone's `Router` class, we can expect that anything passed after `/users/` or `/company/` should be taken care of by the respective subrouter, that is, `App.UsersRouter` or `App.CompanyRouter`.

We can add as many subrouters as we want and the base router won't care about it. Similarly, the subrouters do not know what prefix they have. Any changes in the module name or prefix should be done only in the base router without modifying the related subrouter.

`Backbone.Subroute` is a small yet excellent plugin that you should always include in your application to keep your base router clean. The more modules get added to your application, the more you will understand the benefit of subrouters.

Summary

The functionality of the Backbone router is quite simple and easy to learn. For a simple application, you will not find any problems in maintaining it. The issues will start creeping in once your application grows and your router becomes huge. In this chapter, we discussed the best practices of router management, those that you should always adhere to. We also learned about subrouting, which helps by splitting up the main router into multiple module-specific routers and dividing the tasks among them.

In the next chapter, we will discuss Backbone events, custom events, storages, and sync.

6
Working with Events, Sync, and Storage

In the previous chapters, we discussed each Backbone component (view, model, collection, and router) separately and in detail. In this chapter, we are going to talk about the custom events, `Backbone.sync()` method and `Backbone.LocalStorage`. Though these topics are not exactly related to each other, we placed them in a single chapter as we need to cover each one of them before we move on to application architecture and patterns in the next chapter.

Events are always considered as one of the most powerful concepts in JavaScript. They are a representation of the observer pattern (a well-known design pattern for loose coupling) and are used by most JavaScript libraries. In Backbone, `Backbone.Events` is a nontrivial module that can be used with any object to have event-related functionality. This is how `Backbone.Events` is defined in the Backbone documentation (`http://backbonejs.org/#Events`):

> *Event is a module that can be mixed in to any object, giving the object the ability to bind and trigger custom named events.*

In this chapter, we will discuss why events are important for Backbone application development and how we can use them to achieve higher reusability and a more structured application architecture. The main topics to be covered in this chapter are as follows:

- **Custom events**: Custom events are initialized by an application for a certain purpose that is not served by the base library we are using. We will learn how to create and use custom events in Backbone.

- **Event dispatcher**: Sometimes, we seek an application-level event manager that can work as the centralized tool for event-based communication. Different components of the application can interact with each other via this event manager, without directly communicating among themselves. In this section, we will learn how to create and use such an event dispatcher with our application.

- **Method overriding**: In this topic, we will learn how overriding the sync() method of Backbone lets us create different persistent strategies for public REST APIs or LocalStorage.

- **Offline storage**: The Backbone.LocalStorage adapter can be used with any Backbone model or collection to save the data onto a LocalStorage database.

Understanding custom events

Creating and using custom events are not a big deal in JavaScript—all of the major JavaScript libraries heavily depend on their own events to make their components loosely coupled. Each component possesses a set of custom events for better reusability and integration with the application.

Creating a custom event in Backbone is quite simple—any object that extends the Backbone.Events class gets all of the event-related functionality, that is, listening to, triggering, and removing events. Backbone's View, Model, Collection, and Router are the major components that extend the Backbone.Events class, and you can fire a custom event on any one of them when needed:

```
var myView = new Backbone.View();
myView.on('myevent', function () {
  console.log('"myevent" is fired');
});

myView.trigger('myevent');
```

Here we create a Backbone view instance, register a custom event to it, and fire the event. Once the event is fired, the registered function runs immediately as expected.

Avoid callbacks, use custom events

This heading doesn't imply that you should always use events instead of callback methods. It depends on what the coder intends to achieve, it's absolutely an architectural choice. We intend to discuss this point to understand the cases in which events give much more flexibility than callbacks. Whenever there is a scenario when you need to notify others about a certain condition of any task, you will find that a custom event is a better choice than a callback function. Beginner-level developers often fall into this trap and end up using a callback method, which generally provides a more private and isolated approach.

In the following section, we will demonstrate the necessity of custom events with a simple example.

A simple case study on custom events

Assume we have a `Login` dialog box, and once the user inputs the username-password combination and clicks on the **Submit** button, a request is sent to the server to validate the login. On successful validation, the user closes the dialog box and does some other tasks, such as storing cookies, changing the page title, and so on. In such a case, we generally use a callback method and place all the post-login functionality in it. What if there are 10 different functions each to be called on separate objects once the login is successful? You may need all of these object references within that callback method to call the methods one by one. While this can be achieved without any issue, why not just fire a custom event `loggedin` once the user login is successful? The 10 objects that are already listening to the `loggedin` event can then call the related methods accordingly:

```
var Login = Backbone.View.extend({
  'click #login-btn': 'doLogin',
  doLogin: function () {
    var me = this;

    // send a login request
    $.ajax({
      url: '/login',
      method: 'POST',
      data: {
        username: 'foo',
        password: 'foo'
      },
      success: function (response) {
        me.trigger('loggedin', response);
```

```
        }
    });
  }
});

var loginView = new Login();
login.doLogin();
```

The other components that need to do those post-login tasks should already be listening to the `loggedin` event of that `loginView`, and the callback function will execute as soon as the event is fired:

```
// in some other component
loginView.on('loggedin', function(response){
  // Do something
});
```

You can pass some parameters while triggering the event too; this data will be available in the event callback method as arguments:

```
// Pass multiple data
me.trigger('loggedin', response, 'foo', 'bar');

// All the passed params will be available as function arguments
loginView.on('loggedin', function(response, foo, bar){
  console.log(response, foo, bar);
});
```

Using an event dispatcher

Notice one thing in the previous scenario: to listen to the `loggedin` event, all the other components of the application should have a reference to that `loginView`. Is this really required? It may seem to a few components that keeping a reference to `loginView` is irrelevant, but they have to do so because they need to listen to the `loggedin` event on this `loginView` object. Dependency injection in such a way can be painful even when you are developing a simple application. Sometimes we may need a common object that will play the role of a central event manager and can be used throughout the application to trigger and listen to events. The simplest event dispatcher can be defined in the following way:

```
var vent = _.extend({}, Backbone.Events);

// Listen to a custom event
vent.on('customevent', function(){
```

```
    console.log('Custom event fired');
});

// Fire the event
vent.trigger('customevent');
```

When we make the vent variable available at the application-level, it can work as a centralized event dispatcher to publish and subscribe to events. This pattern is called PubSub pattern and is quite beneficial for use in a module- or widget-based application architecture.

 You should understand the context where this will be a good choice. An event dispatcher should be used when you either have too many components to listen to (as we saw in the case of the login example) or when you have some completely unrelated objects that need to communicate with each other.

The main problem that you may face while working with a common event dispatcher is that the number of publishers and subscribers may get out of control when too many events are registered through a single event dispatcher. For example, say we have two modules, User and Company, and both the modules are subscribed to an event named addcomment on the event dispatcher separately; they are defined as follows:

```
vent.on('addcomment', user.addComment);
vent.on('addcomment', company.addComment);
```

Notice that the event name is the same, but the functions to be called are different. So, if you want another subscriber to be notified for the same event, you need to clear up all the other subscribers of that event first and then publish the event. However, there are a few other simple solutions to this issue, such as creating multiple event dispatchers or using different event namespaces.

Creating multiple event dispatchers

Defining a separate event dispatcher for individual modules or functionality can provide a solution to the problem we described previously:

```
App.userVent = _.extend({}, Backbone.Events);
App.documentVent = extend({}, Backbone.Events);
```

Now, the same event names for different dispatchers will never clash:

```
App.userVent.on('addcomment', user.addComment);
App.documentVent.on('addcomment', company.addComment);
```

Using different event namespaces

This is as simple as following a specific naming convention while using custom events:

```
App.vent.trigger('before:login');
App.vent.trigger('after:login');
App.vent.trigger('user:add:comment');
```

Adding a colon in the event name doesn't make the event special, but makes it different and unique because it now relates to some specific modules of the application. This is a convention heavily used by JavaScript developers and we encourage you to use it whenever required.

Avoiding memory leaks with the listenTo() method

Memory management is a very important part of any application. Generally, for frontend development, developers do not bother much about memory leaks; however, this doesn't hold true when we develop single page frontend-heavy applications. These types of applications deal with many frontend components and the lowest number of page refreshes, which can create several opportunities for memory leaks. While developing such applications, we should always be careful to clean up events when an object is destroyed. To understand this with an example, assume we have a view that displays its model's data. The render() method of the view is called whenever the change event is fired on that model:

```
// Memory leak
var MyView = Backbone.View.extend({
  tpl: '<%= name %>',
  model: new Backbone.Model({
    name: 'Suramya'
  }),

  initialize: function () {
    this.model.on('change', this.render, this);
  },

  render: function () {
    var html = _.template(this.tpl, this.model.toJSON());
    this.$el.html(html);
```

```
      return this;
    }
});

var myView = new MyView();
$(document.body).append(myView.render().el);

myView.model.set('name', 'Arup');
myView.remove();
```

Now, as you can see, we registered a `change` event on the model so that whenever any of its attributes change, the `render` method will be called. Then we created an instance of the view, changed the `name` attribute of the model, and destroyed the view. The `remove()` method destroys the `view` instance and removes the view from the DOM.

The whole process works as expected, though with a slight problem. When you create a view in JavaScript, you create DOM nodes and bind event listeners to them. When you remove nodes from the DOM, their event listeners hold references to them. As a result, your JavaScript engine will not automatically garbage collect the nodes as there are still references to them in the scope. In our case too, even if the view is destroyed, the `change` event listener on the model persists and we need to take care of it explicitly. How can we do this? We can add a `close()` method to the view and unbind all such events in this method before destroying the view:

```
close: function () {
  this.model.off('change', this.render, this);
  this.remove();
}
```

Now everything is cleaned up properly. But do we need to keep doing this for all of our views? No, because Backbone V9.9 introduced a `listenTo()` method that tells an object to listen to an event of another object:

```
this.listenTo(this.model, 'change', this.render);
```

This works exactly the same way, but the advantage of this over the `on()` method is that it allows the object to keep track of events, and they can be removed all at once later on. So, we will not need an extra `close()` method to unbind all the events before destroying the view. Rather, the `remove()` method of Backbone view will now clean up any bound event by calling the `stopListening()` method.

So, use the `on()` method when you want to take care of the handler yourself and where scenarios like event cleanup or zombie handling will not arise. Otherwise, go for `listenTo()`, which we will mostly find useful in the context of Backbone views.

Overriding the Backbone.sync() method

Backbone provides a single gateway for all its data communication. All the data requests are sent via the `sync()` method that gets called whenever any CRUD operation is processed. This `sync()` method does a number of jobs, such as setting the URL, parameters and content type, and mimicking HTTP requests for old browsers that do not support PUT and DELETE requests. Whenever we call a `fetch()` or `save()` method on a model or collection, the `sync()` method is executed.

But when do we need to override this method? Sometimes, you may need a separate implementation of the REST API method, which Backbone does not provide. This can be for a certain model or collection, or the implementation can persist for the complete project. This is how the method map is written in Backbone by default:

```
var methodMap = {
  'create': 'POST',
  'update': 'PUT',
  'patch': 'PATCH',
  'delete': 'DELETE',
  'read': 'GET'
};
```

Now, you may have a particular model or collection that will listen to a separate API other than the default one, say the Google or Twitter API, which you cannot change. Or, you may want to implement an offline storage that will use the browser's local storage to operate on the data. In such cases, you need to override the `sync()` method of that collection or model, or if it is common throughout the application, you need to override the `Backbone.sync()` method. Let's understand its importance with an example. Here we want our `User` module to interact directly with the public API `FooApi`:

```
// FooApi is a public api with 'add', 'edit', 'read'
// and 'delete' methods
var User = Backbone.Model.extend({
  sync: function (method, model, options) {
    options || (options = {});

    switch (method) {
    case 'create':
```

```
          FooApi.add(options.data);
          break;

       case 'update':
         FooApi.edit(options.data);
         break;

       case 'delete':
         FooApi.delete({
            id: options.data.id
         });
         break;

       case 'read':
         FooApi.read({
            id: options.data.id
         });
         break;
       }
       // Other stuff
   }
});

var user = new User({
   name: 'Manali',
   age: 29
});

// This will call FooApi.add() method
user.save();
```

Look how we used a `switch` case to call the `FooApi` method for each of the data operation methods. Now, when you call the `save()` method on the user instance, it will call the `FooApi.add()` method directly. You can use the other data operations similarly. So, this is the way in which Backbone's `sync()` method is overridden to create a wrapper that maps the models and methods of another API.

Offline storage using the Backbone.LocalStorage adapter

In the previous section, we saw how overriding the `Backbone.sync()` method provides you with customized data operations, including models and collections. Most of the time, we use the HTML5 `LocalStorage` functionality to store our data in the browser for offline browsing. This is a pretty common requirement for storing small data in a browser while developing mobile websites and mobile web applications. The `LocalStorage` communication can also be done with the help of the `sync()` method in a way that is exactly the same as the technique used in the previous section by overriding the `sync()` method.

Rather than creating this solution ourselves, we will look into an excellent adapter, `Backbone.LocalStorage` (http://documentup.com/jeromegn/backbone.localStorage), which was developed by Jerome Gravel-Niquet and widely used by the Backbone.js developer community for interacting with `LocalStorage`. This adapter can be plugged into any model or collection, and thus enables them to communicate with `LocalStorage` using the `save()` or `fetch()` methods as follows:

```
var Users = Backbone.Collection.extend({
  model: Backbone.Model,
  localStorage: new Backbone.LocalStorage("users")
});

var users = new Users();

// Add items to collection
users.add([{
  name: 'Soumendu De'
}, {
  name: 'Bikash Debroy'
}])

// Sync collection data to localstorage
users.each(function (user) {
  user.save();
});
```

Here we defined a collection by passing an instance of `Backbone.LocalStorage` to the `LocalStorage` property. This is the only configuration that is requires to attach the collection to `LocalStorage` and perform all of the data operations on it. Also, this configuration works for both the model and the collection. If you want to know how the `sync()` functionality has been implemented within this adapter, go ahead and look into the adapter code—it's small and pretty well-written.

Another popular `LocalStorage` adapter is `Backbone.dualStorage` (`https://github.com/nilbus/Backbone.dualStorage`). There are quite a few adapters available online and all of them provide a similar functionality. So, if you want to follow some tool other than the one we mentioned, you are free to do so.

Summary

Events in JavaScript are one of the most interesting concepts; lots of articles and books are available on this subject. We didn't try to look into all the details in this chapter, but we analyzed how using custom events and an event dispatcher in your Backbone application can provide enormous flexibility and scalability to the application architecture. We encourage you to explore JavaScript events, function scopes, and an event dispatcher or PubSub pattern if you need a more detailed idea about it.

In this chapter, we also learned about Backbone's `sync()` method and how we can override the `sync()` method to get custom data operations for public APIs or the HTML5 `LocalStorage`.

Also, we have looked at various components of Backbone and discussed their best practices, few plugins and extensions related to them, and some common issues. In the next chapter, we will see how we can organize Backbone applications with different design patterns and architecture.

7
Organizing Backbone Applications – Structure, Optimize, and Deploy

In the previous chapters of this book, we looked at the individual components of Backbone.js and learned about several good practices that help create a better application. However, Backbone itself doesn't provide any application structure or guidance on how to organize the application source code. This makes it quite difficult for beginner-level programmers to understand how to create a folder structure, add proper namespaces, load script files in the appropriate order, and follow patterns to create a robust app architecture.

Almost every Backbone.js developer, at some point of time, faces this issue. You can find many articles (check the blog links on application architecture in *Appendix A, Books, Tutorials, and References*) on the Web where developers have described how they tried to structure their Backbone code base. But that again makes the task difficult because you may need to choose a particular solution from a number of different opinions and understand whether that is the best solution or not. In this chapter, we will look at a step-by-step process on how to organize the structure for both small- and large-scale applications.

- **Application directory structure**: Code organization is crucial in order to start developing a nontrivial JavaScript application. This section illustrates a boilerplate directory structure that may help you to conceptualize your application structure.

- **Asynchronous module definition**: Rather than stacking a number of JavaScript files in your HTML file, **Asynchronous Module Definition (AMD)** helps in defining modules and loading its dependencies asynchronously in a subtle way.

- **Application architecture**: This section provides a complete step-by-step guide on the patterns and best practices that you should follow in your application architecture to make it flexible and maintainable.

Understanding the application directory structure

Code organization in a filesystem plays an important role in application development. It provides solutions to several problems such as the following:

- Managing the separation of concern for views, models, collections, and routers
- Defining a clear entry point to the application
- Proper namespacing

The directory structure that we are going to propose here is not something that will work universally for every application. As JavaScript doesn't provide an inherent code organization mechanism, there is no single pattern that is best for all the applications; it solely depends on the situation. You are free to use the following structure, and lots of developers use it for their projects without any issues:

```
App Directory Structure


|-- app
|   |-- models
|   |   |-- user.js
|   |-- collections
|   |   |-- users.js
|   |-- routers
|   |   |-- app.js
|   |-- views
|   |   |-- users
|   |   |   |-- list.js
|   |   |   |-- add.js
|   |-- utils
|   |   |-- utility.js
|   |-- main.js
|   |-- app.js
|-- libs
|   |-- jquery.js
|   |-- backbone
|   |   |-- backbone.js
|   |-- underscore
|   |   |-- underscore.js
|-- assets            // all static resources go here
|   |-- images
|   |-- css
|-- templates         // will hold all the template files
|   |-- login.html
|   |-- users
|   |   |-- list.html
|   |   |-- add.html
|-- test              // Includes the test files
|-- config            // config files
|-- mixins            // mixin files
|-- index.html
```

We kept all of the static assets inside the `assets` folder. You can add more folders if you have other types of static resources. The templates are stored in a separate directory that matches the `views` folder structure. We will load these templates dynamically as needed and optimize them later to create a single file with all the templates (refer to *Appendix C, Organizing Templates with AMD and Require.js*, for more details). The `main.js` file is the entry point of the application. You will see its usage in the following section when we will discuss working with AMD. The `app.js` file holds the application class that acts as the topmost parent class of the application. All the utility files such as `utility.js` or `helper.js`, which mostly contain the helper methods, sit in the `util` folder. The `test` folder is the main directory in which all the test scripts are stored. The `config` and `mixin` folders are there to store the config and reusable mixin files respectively. This file structure is basic and can work as the boilerplate of your application.

There is another pattern that became popular for large and complex applications recently—the modular approach. In this case, we divide the complete application into multiple small modules; each module will add a specific functionality to the app. We will look into it later in this chapter, but we can discuss the file structure of this pattern here. A module consists of its own views, models, and collections. You can have one `templates` folder for each module and place that module's templates separately in that folder, or you can leave it as it is as a single `templates` folder for the complete project. We will go for the latter; the `app` folder will look like the following screenshot:

```
Modular App Directory Structure

|-- app
|    |-- modules            // all modules reside here
|    |    |-- user
|    |    |    |-- models
|    |    |    |-- collections
|    |    |    |-- views
|    |    |    |-- main.js   // main.js is the entry point of module
|    |    |-- payment
|    |-- utils
|    |-- main.js
|    |-- app.js
```

As you can see, there is no separate `models`, `collections`, or `views` folder; instead, there is a `modules` directory that includes all the modules of the application. Each module contains a `main.js` file that works as the starting point of that module.

Now, how will you benefit by using such a modular pattern over the directory structure? Actually this is not just a change in the directory structure, but a completely new application architecture. We noticed that beginner-level developers, who are not very familiar with the module patterns, find it difficult to start with this structure—probably because it's a new concept. However, once you start using it, you will realize that it is quite easy to work with and flexible too. The advantages of using such structures are as follows:

- The modules are generally independent of each other. So, you can re-use one module elsewhere with minimum changes.

- The modules generally do not communicate with each other directly; they use a common medium to communicate. So, you can change or delete one module while the others stay untouched.

- Your code base becomes modular and more flexible as each module encapsulates their functionality. For example, a `User` module performs all of the user-related functions; no other part of your application will handle any user-related job.

The previous structure is not the only way to make the app modular. There are several other concepts and you can choose any of them as per your requirements. For example, I often use the AuraJS directory structure (the `TodoMVC` app from `https://github.com/aurajs/todomvc`) while working with this framework. It is similar yet different and useful. So, if you are aware of multiple such directory structures and do not know which one to choose, go for the one that we mentioned previously. There is no harm in following a standard structure; it is better than going for an unstructured project directory.

Working with Asynchronous Module Definition

So far, we have learned to add all our script files in HTML files within `SCRIPT` tags. The browser loads these files synchronously and hence we always need to ensure that if one file has a dependency over another file, the latter should always be loaded prior to the former. Since all of the references to these dependencies are made via global variables, these dependencies must be loaded in the proper order, and a developer must take care of them before he adds a new script file to the application. Although this process works just fine, it may become difficult to manage large applications as too many dependencies will overlap. AMD provides a solution to this problem.

AMD is a mechanism used to define a module such that the module and its dependencies can be asynchronously loaded. So, multiple AMD modules can be loaded in parallel, and once the last dependent module is loaded, the main module will execute. In addition, AMD omits the use of global variables by encapsulating the module definition, and provides a way to load multiple modules into one file and obviates the need for explicit namespacing.

Presently, the most popular script loader that supports AMD is Require.js (`http://requirejs.org`). It provides an implementation of the module patterns and allows us to create a centrally-managed dependency mapping using its map configuration. Discussing Require.js in detail is beyond the scope of this chapter. So, if you want to get a complete overview of the concept, we recommend you visit their website first before proceeding to the following sections.

Adding Require.js to your project

While `require.js` loads all the modules of your application, it is the only file that you need to include in your `index.html` file. Add the following script tag within the `HEAD` tag:

```
<script data-main="app/main" src="libs/require.js"></script>
```

The `data-main` attribute specifies the JavaScript file that will act as the starting point of the application. In this case, it is our `main.js` file. Once the `require.js` file is loaded, it looks into the `data-main` attribute's entry point and loads that script. We are going to add the entire `require.js` configuration to this file along with all of the libraries and their dependencies. You do not need to add a `.js` extension to any file as RequireJS automatically appends that.

Configuring dependencies

We are going to add all the library files in the RequireJS config option, along with their paths and dependencies, to the `main.js` file:

```
// File: app/main.js

require.config({
  baseUrl: 'libs',
  paths: {
    jquery: 'jquery',
    underscore: 'underscore/underscore',
    backbone: 'backbone/backbone'
  },
  shim: {
```

```
    // We assume the backbone file here is a non-AMD file
    backbone: {
      exports: 'Backbone',
      deps: ['underscore', 'jquery']
    }
  }
});
```

We call the `require.config()` method in the `data-main` entry file and pass a configuration object with a set of properties to it. There are quite a number of properties that can go as config options, but we will discuss only those that are the most important at this point. You can find a complete list in the `require.js` API (http://requirejs.org/docs/api.html):

- `baseUrl`: This config defines the root path so you do not need to include it every time in your file paths.

- `paths`: This config specifies the shortcut alias of each file and the paths to the files are given relative to `baseUrl`.

- `shim`: This config should be used only for the non-AMD files, that is, the scripts that do not already call the `define()` method. It will not work properly for AMD files.

- `exports`: This config is the global variable name of that module.

- `deps`: This config is an array of dependencies that must be loaded first before the respective module loads.

You need to look for the AMD-enabled version of the library files if you want to use them directly. Otherwise, you have to go via the `shim` option.

Defining a module

RequireJS provides two important methods — `define()` and `require()`, which facilitate module definition and dependency loading respectively. The `define()` method takes an optional module ID, an optional array that includes the dependencies that this module may require, and a function that gets executed in order to instantiate the module. The most basic module definition of a Backbone model will look like this:

```
// File: app/models/user.js

define([
    'jquery',
    'underscore',
    'backbone'
```

```
  ],
  function ($, _, Backbone) {
    var User = Backbone.Model.extend({
      defaults: ['name', 'age']
    });
    return User;
  });
```

Now, this model can be used in another file just as the other dependencies. The interesting thing is that RequireJS makes sure that a particular file is loaded only once, irrespective of how many times you include it in several files. Now, let's create a `Users` collection and use our `User` model there:

```
// File: app/collections/users.js

define(function (require) {
  var $ = require('jquery'),
    _ = require('underscore'),
    Backbone = require('backbone'),
    UserModel = require('app/models/user');

  var Users = Backbone.Collection.extend({
    model: UserModel
  });

  return Users;
});
```

It is pretty simple, right? Also, notice that we loaded the dependencies in a pattern other than what we used for our model definition. This pattern is called the `Sugar` syntax and it utilizes the `require()` method to load the dependencies. You can use either of the syntaxes with your module definitions. When there are lots of dependencies, using the `Sugar` syntax makes it easier to organize the dependency variables rather than just putting them as arguments of a function.

So, with AMD, you can define all of your files in the same way. The script dependencies are loaded as we saw previously, and the text dependencies can be loaded using the `text` plugin (`https://github.com/requirejs/text`) of RequireJS. We already discussed this thoroughly in *Appendix C, Organizing Templates with AMD and Require.js*, when we loaded the external template files using this plugin. In the following section, we are going to see how we can initiate a complete application architecture using these concepts.

Creating application architecture

The essential premise at the heart of Backbone has always been to try and discover the minimal set of data-structuring (Models and Collections) and user interface (Views and URLs) primitives that are useful when building web applications with JavaScript.

Jeremy Ashkenas, creator of Backbone.js, Underscore.js, and CoffeeScript

As Jeremy mentioned, Backbone.js has no intention, at least in the near future, to raise its bar to provide application architecture. Backbone will continue to be a lightweight tool to produce the minimal features required for web development. So, should we blame Backbone.js for not including such functionality even though there is a huge demand for this in the developer community? Certainly not! Backbone.js only yields the set of components that are necessary to create the backbone of an application and gives us complete freedom to build the app architecture in whichever way we want.

If working on a significantly large JavaScript application, remember to dedicate sufficient time to planning the underlying architecture that makes the most sense. It's often more complex than you may initially imagine.

Addy Osmani, author of Patterns For Large-Scale JavaScript Application Architecture

So, as we start digging into more detail on creating an application architecture, we are not going to talk about trivial applications or something similar to a to-do-list app. Rather, we will investigate how to structure a medium- or large-level application. After discussions with a number of developers, we found that the main issue they face here is that there are several methodologies the online blog posts and tutorials offer to structure an application. While most of these tutorials talk about good practices, it becomes difficult to choose exactly one from them. Keeping that in mind, we will explore a number of steps that you should follow to make your app robust and maintainable in the long run.

Managing a project directory

This is the first step towards creating a solid app architecture. We have already discussed this in detail in the previous sections. If you are comfortable using another directory layout, go ahead with it. The directory structure will not matter much if the rest of your application is organized properly.

Organizing code with AMD

We will use RequireJS for our project. As discussed earlier, it comes with a bunch of facilities such as the following:

- Adding a lot of script tags in one HTML file and managing all of the dependencies on your own may work for a medium-level project, but will gradually fail for a large-level project. Such a project may have thousands of lines of code; managing a code base of that size requires small modules to be defined in each individual file. With RequireJS, you do not need to worry about how many files you have—you just know that if the standard is followed properly, it is bound to work.

- The global namespace is never touched and you can freely give the best names to something that matches with it the most.

- Debugging the RequireJS modules is a lot easier than other approaches because you know what the dependencies and path to each of them are in every module definition.

- You can use `r.js`, an optimization tool for RequireJS that minifies all the JavaScript and CSS files, to create the production-ready build.

Setting up an application

For a Backbone app, there must be a centralized object that will hold together all the components of the application. In a simple application, most people generally just make the main router work as the central object. But that will surely not work for a large application and you need an `Application` object that should work as the parent component. This object should have a method (mostly `init()`) that will work as the entry point to your application and initialize the main router along with the Backbone history. In addition, either your `Application` class should extend `Backbone.Events` or it should include a property that points to an instance of the `Backbone.Events` class. The benefit of doing this is that the `app` or `Backbone.Events` instance can act as a central event aggregator, and you can trigger application-level events on it.

A very basic `Application` class will look like the following code snippet:

```
// File: application.js

define([
  'underscore',
  'backbone',
  'router'
], function (_, Backbone, Router) {
  // the event aggregator
```

```
    var PubSub = _.extend({}, Backbone.Events);

    var Application = function () {
      // Do useful stuff here
    }

    _.extend(Application.prototype, {
      pubsub: new PubSub(),
      init: function () {
        Backbone.history.start();
      }
    });

    return Application;
  });
```

`Application` is a simple class with an `init()` method and a `PubSub` instance. The `init()` method acts as the starting point of the application and `PubSub` works as the application-level event manager. You can add more functionality to the `Application` class, such as starting and stopping modules and adding a region manager for view layout management. It is advisable to keep this class as short as you can.

Using the module pattern

We often see that intermediate-level developers find it a bit confusing to initially use a module-based architecture. It can be a little difficult for them to make the transition from a simple MVC architecture to a modular MVC architecture. While the points we are discussing in this chapter are valid for both these architectures, we should always prefer to use a modular concept in nontrivial applications for better maintainability and organization.

In the directory structure section, we saw how the module consists of a `main.js` file, its views, models, and collections all together. The `main.js` file will define the module and have different methods to manage the other components of that module. It works as the starting point of the module. A simple `main.js` file will look like the following code:

```
// File: main.js

define([
  'app/modules/user/views/userlist',
```

```
      'app/modules/user/views/userdetails'
], function (UserList, UserDetails) {
  var myVar;

  return {
    initialize: function () {
      this.showUserList();
  },

    showUsersList: function () {
      var userList = new UserList();
      userList.show();
    },

    showUserDetails: function (userModel) {
      var userDetails = new UserDetails({
        model: userModel
      });
      userDetails.show();
    }
  };
});
```

As you can see, the responsibility of this file is to initiate the module and manage the components of that module. We have to make sure that it handles only parent-level tasks; it shouldn't contain a method that one of its views should ideally have.

The concept is not very complex, but you need to set it up properly in order to use it for a large application. You can even go for an existing app and module setup and integrate it with your Backbone app. For instance, Marionette provides an application infrastructure for Backbone apps. You can use its inbuilt Application and Module classes to structure your application. It also provides a general-purpose Controller class—something that doesn't come with the Backbone library but can be used as a mediator to provide generic methods and work as a common medium among the modules.

You can also use AuraJS (https://github.com/aurajs/aura), a framework-agonistic event-driven architecture developed by Addy Osmani (http://addyosmani.com) and many others; it works quite well with Backbone.js. A thorough discussion on AuraJS is beyond the scope of this book, but you can grab a lot of useful information about it from its documentation and examples (https://github.com/aurajs/todomvc). It is an excellent boilerplate tool that gives your app a kick-start and we highly recommend it, especially if you are not using the Marionette application infrastructure. The following are a few benefits of using AuraJS; they may help you choose this framework for your application:

- AuraJS is framework-agnostic. Though it works great with Backbone.js, you can use it for your JavaScript module architecture even if you aren't using Backbone.js.

- It utilizes the module pattern, application-level and module-level communication using the facade (sandbox) and mediator patterns.

- It abstracts away the utility libraries that you use (such as templating and DOM manipulation) so you can swap alternatives anytime you want.

Managing objects and module communication

One of the most important ways to keep the application code maintainable is to reduce the tight coupling between modules and objects. If you are following the module pattern, you should never let one module communicate with another directly. Loose coupling adds a level of restriction in your code, and a change in one module will never enforce a change in the rest of the application. Moreover, it lets you re-use the same modules elsewhere. But how can we communicate if there is no direct relationship? The two important patterns we use in this case are the observer and mediator patterns.

Using the observer/PubSub pattern

The PubSub pattern is nothing but the event dispatcher concept that we discussed in *Chapter 6, Working with Events, Sync, and Storage*. It works as a messaging channel between the object (publisher) that fires the event and another object (subscriber) that receives the notification.

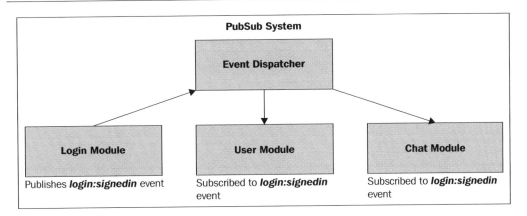

We mentioned earlier that we can have an application-level event aggregator as a property of the `Application` object. This event aggregator can work as the common channel via which the other modules can communicate, and that too without interacting directly.

Even at the module-level, you may need a common event dispatcher only for that module; the views, models, and collections of that module can use it to communicate with each other. However, publishing too many events via a dispatcher sometimes makes it difficult to manage them and you must be careful enough to understand which events you should publish via a generic dispatcher and which ones you should fire on a certain component only. Anyhow, this pattern is one of the best tools to design a decoupled system, and you should always have one ready for use in your module-based application.

Using the mediator pattern

Sometimes, you may find that too many relationships exist between the modules of your app, and you need a central point of control that will help manage all the communication. This centralized system is called the mediator; it works as a *shared subject* between a set of modules and promotes loose coupling by not referring to the modules explicitly. All the modules will have a reference to this mediator.

The mediator pattern is somewhat similar to the observer pattern, but it doesn't work as a broadcasting system. It includes a set of methods that are accessible to all modules that share this mediator. A mediator can be a simple object with a number of required methods:

```
var Mediator = {
  method1: function(){},
  method2: function(){}
};
```

Any module can access any method of this mediator.

> *A mediator is best applied when two or more objects have an indirect working relationship, and business logic or workflow needs to dictate the interactions and coordination of these objects.*

> *Addy Osmani*

The concept of a mediator will get more clear once we look at a simple example. Assume that we have two modules: User and Event. The User module has a getUserDetails() method to retrieve a user's details based on the user ID. The Event module has a loadEvents() method whose job it is to load all the events near the user's current location. Now, getting the currently logged-in user's ID or current location is a functionality that isn't particularly module-specific, and it is better to keep it in a Mediator instance. Look at the following example:

```
// Mediator
define(['util'], function (Util) {
  var Mediator = {
    getLoggedinUser: function () {
      return Util.getCookie('userid');
    },

    getUserCurrentLocation: function () {
      // returns user's current location
    }
  };

  return Mediator;
});

// User module
define(['app/mediator'],
  function (Mediator) {
```

```
    var User = function () {};

    User.prototype.getUserDetails = function () {
      var userId = Mediator.getLoggedinUser();

      // Load user's details with the loggedin user id
    }

    return User;
  });

// Event module
define(['app/mediator'],
  function (Mediator) {
    var Event = function () {};

    Event.prototype.loadEvents = function () {
      var userLocation = Mediator.getUserCurrentLocation();

      // load events nearby user's location
    }

    Event.prototype.showEventDetails = function () {}

    return Event;
  });
```

As you can see, we just pass the `Mediator` instance in both the module definitions and place the reusable and shared methods inside the mediator so that they can be accessed from any module. This is a basic example; we hope that it conveys the idea of using a mediator. In a complete application level, a mediator may take care of a lot of its functionality. Using a mediator without knowing its proper use is not a good idea—let's look at the pros and cons of using a mediator pattern:

- The pros are as follows:
    - The biggest advantage of using the mediator pattern is that it enforces the communication channel between modules to change from many-to-many to many-to-one. So, the modules will not communicate directly with each other but via the `mediator` object.
    - It omits the tight coupling between modules and thus reduces the architectural complexity in large applications.

- The cons are as follows:
  - ○ The main drawback of this pattern is that it can introduce a single point of failure.
  - ○ Communicating back and forth via a mediator may sometimes result in a performance hit.

Anyhow, both these patterns—observer and mediator, if you have noticed already, are one of the simplest to implement. If used properly, they can become the best resources for organizing and maintaining your application. It is not a big deal to use them; you can implement these concepts even in small- and medium-level applications. Whenever you feel the need for module or component communication, a mediator or PubSub pattern can become handy.

Understanding view management

Backbone views are very lightweight components, and you need to add some custom functions to handle event binding, proper layout, data integration, and life cycle management in almost every app. So, it is always preferable to have a base view that will handle this common functionality; all other views will extend from it. For this purpose, we recommend you choose MarionetteJS, which provides three extremely useful view classes: `ItemView`, `CollectionView`, and `CompositeView`. These classes, along with Marionette's base `View` class, facilitate the most important boilerplate functionality that one may need to use for his/her app views.

There are two more important aspects of view management: the layout manager and the template handler. We discussed both these topics in detail in *Chapter 2, Working with Views*. In a large application, a single page consists of multiple views and a major task involves creating, switching, and destroying these views. While you can always handle this layout management yourself, an existing robust layout manager will help you to maintain these views and clean up the memory. You can choose either the `Backbone.LayoutManager` plugin or the `Marionette.RegionManager` extension for this job. Both of them provide similar functionality and are well-accepted in the developer community.

For templates, we advise you to observe the following important points for a large application:

- Use Handlebars instead of Underscore's template engine, although there is no restriction in choosing other template engines. Just make sure that you do not evaluate JavaScript code in your template—this increases the complexity, as we discussed in *Chapter 2, Working with Views*.

- Keep your view templates in separate and individual files.

- Always precompile your templates. A number of processes that we discussed in *Chapter 2, Working with Views, Appendix B, Precompiling Templates on the Server Side*, and *Appendix C, Organizing Templates with AMD and Require.js*, describe how you should precompile your templates and load them.

Understanding other important features

There are few more things that you need to take care of while developing complex apps. They are as follows:

- **Multiple routers**: It's always preferable to have multiple routers compared to a gigantic router class. We discussed the concept of subrouters in *Chapter 5, Routing Best Practices and Subrouting*.

- **Utility methods**: Each application needs a set of utility methods that are generic and can be used by any component of the application. You should always have one or more than one `Utility` class depending on the requirements, and these classes should take care of all the common utility methods.

- **DOM handling**: The more you interact with the DOM in your views, the more difficult will it be to maintain in the later stage. Always try to reduce direct DOM manipulation as much as you can.

- **Error handler**: Keep a generic error/exception handler ready; it should work as a single point for the errors/warnings and display messages to the users.

- **Memory management**: In single-page large applications, memory leak is a real point of concern. So, you must be very much careful about not initiating global variables, cleaning up references when they are not in use, and unbinding events when the related element or component is removed.

Summary

This chapter dealt with one of the most important topics of Backbone.js-based application development. At the framework level, learning Backbone is quite easy and developers get a complete grasp over it in a very short period of time. Developing simple applications with a few pages never seems to be an issue. But when it comes to a large complex application, laying out the architecture becomes quite confusing, with what to include and what not to. In this chapter, we tried to discuss every point associated with the app's architecture and mentioned when and why you should use a particular pattern. Moreover, most of these patterns are applied to a number of large applications with success. So, you can adopt these concepts without any hesitation.

Until this chapter, we talked about almost everything related to Backbone.js application development. However, no project is complete without proper testing, and that is what we are going to learn in our next and final chapter, *Chapter 8, Unit Test, Stub, Spy, and Mock Your App.*

8
Unit Test, Stub, Spy, and Mock Your App

Majority of developers believe that testing is essential, but in reality only a few of them actually go for test-driven development. Testing falls under one of the best practices of the JavaScript development process. Hence, we decided to include a chapter on how to unit test Backbone-based applications.

A number of popular testing libraries, such as QUnit, Jasmine, Mocha, and SinonJS, are available to unit test JavaScript applications. In this chapter, we are going to show you how to test with QUnit, the simplest yet robust testing platform, which is pretty easy to learn as well. In the latter part, we will look into SinonJS to learn test spies, stubs, and mocks. Together, QUnit and SinonJS create a strong tool to test every part of your app. The main points to be discussed in this chapter are as follows:

- **Why unit testing is important**: Testing is a habit. Continuing this along with development may take some extra time initially, but it is essential especially while working in a team or developing complex applications.

- **Testing with QUnit**: We will look into the basic aspects of QUnit, and we will see how to use them for the Backbone.js components.

- **Using spies, stubs, and mocks with SinonJS**: Spying on the behavior of JavaScript functions and controlling their behavior whenever needed from a test environment is absolutely necessary for unit testing. We will look into this concept briefly with the SinonJS test framework.

Understanding why unit testing is important

If you already know the benefits of testing and follow the best practices while developing your JavaScript apps, you can skip this section. If you still wonder why you should actually test your application while you are already writing clean and maintainable code, the following are a few reasons to consider:

- Testing is never a waste of time. You do not need to run your code repeatedly to see whether it works or not. You can run all the test cases at once to see whether everything is functioning as expected. Testing gives you the confidence that your code is working fine.

- Unit tests are really fast to create and fast to run too.

- Update your code without worry. Your test will tell you whether the function is working as it is expected to or not. You will find this very helpful, especially when you work in a team.

- Once you start writing unit tests for your code, you will soon find that you are writing more modular, flexible, and testable code than you used to.

- In **Test Driven Development** (TDD), you write failing test cases first and then develop the code. In that case, a passing test case ensures that your developed code works fine without any issues.

Testing is fun. It's not very easy, sure, and not something that you can master in a day. It is not very difficult either—lots of developers are doing it and you can do it too.

Testing with QUnit

QUnit (`http://qunitjs.com`), a lightweight unit testing framework maintained by the jQuery team, which is quite easy to work with compared to other frameworks. Discussing QUnit in complete detail is beyond the scope of this book, but we will learn about the simple features of it and explore how we can use it with our Backbone components.

Assertions are the most essential elements of any unit test framework. You need to compare your actual implementation values to the results that the test produces. Assertions are the methods that serve this comparison functionality. QUnit has only eight assertions; we are going to use some of them in the next section. Let's discuss a few of them here:

- `ok (state, message)`: This passes if the first argument is true

- `equal (actual, expected, message)`: This returns true if `actual` and `expected` are equal

- `deepEqual (actual, expected, message)`: This is a deep recursive-comparison assertion, working on primitive types, arrays, objects, regular expressions, dates, and functions

- `strictEqual (actual, expected, message)`: This is a strict type and a value comparison assertion

- `throws (block, actual, message)`: This is an assertion to test whether a callback throws an exception when run

There are few more asserts: `notEqual()`, `notDeepEqual()`, and `notStrictEqual()`. The functionalities of these are clearly the opposite of their counterparts. In addition to these, `QUnit` has a number of test methods that are used to initiate the tests. They are as follows:

- `asyncTest()`: This adds an asynchronous test to run

- `expect()`: This specifies how many assertions are expected to run within a test

- `module()`: This consists of group-related tests under a single label

- `test()`: This adds a test to run

Setting up `QUnit` is fairly straightforward. First we will create a `test` directory and put it inside our project directory. This `test` folder is going to hold all our test files of the project. Then, inside this folder, we will create an HTML file, which will show all the test results in our browser. In general, `QUnit` comes up with `qunit.js` and a `qunit.css` files. You need to just include the following code snippet as given in the QUnit website (`http://qunitjs.com`) in your HTML file and you are done with the QUnit setup:

```
<!DOCTYPE html>
<html>
<head>
  <meta charset="utf-8">
  <title>QUnit Example</title>
  <link rel="stylesheet" href="/resources/qunit.css">
</head>
<body>
  <div id="qunit"></div>
  <div id="qunit-fixture"></div>
  <script src="/resources/qunit.js"></script>
  <script src="/resources/tests.js"></script>
</body>
</html>
```

The `tests.js` file will hold all your test cases. You can have multiple test files depending on your requirements. If you found that this section is a little complex and it is difficult to understand all the definitions of assertion methods, do not worry. In the next section, we will show you a simple `QUnit` test case with few of these assertions, and you will see how easy it is to get started with `QUnit`.

Performing a basic test case

We learned the basic and important API methods of `QUnit`. Now, let's use few of them to create a simple test case. We will write a method that checks whether a number is prime or not. Then we will make a couple of calls to the `isPrime()` method from our test and analyze the results as follows:

```
// Function to check a prime number
function isPrime(number) {
  var start = 2;
  while (start <= Math.sqrt(number)) {
    if (number % start++ < 1) return false;
  }
  return number > 1;
}

test('Test a prime number', function () {
  // tells you how many assertions are there in the test
  expect(2);

  // following two assertions check with two numbers
  // whether they are prime number or not
  ok(isPrime(3), '3 is a prime number');
  equal(isPrime(8), false, '8 is not a prime number');
});
```

A rather simple example is shared in the previous code snippet to show how easy it is to get started with `QUnit`. We use the `expect()` method at first to assure that we will be doing two assertions in this test case. If we do more than two assertions, then this test will fail. Now, those two asserts, namely `ok()` and `equal()`, call the `isPrime()` method with two different inputs and check whether those input values are prime numbers or not. When you run this test, you can see both the tests to pass through.

Understanding the QUnit module (), setup (), and teardown () methods

To organize multiple test cases, we need something that can provide a block structure and hold multiple tests together. The `module()` method allows us to group the test cases together. Furthermore, it introduces the two methods, `setup()` and `teardown()`, that run before and after each test case, as shown in the following code snippet:

```
// First module
module('1st module', {
  setup: function () {
    // Runs before each test
  },
  teardown: function () {
    // Runs after each test
  }
});
test('Test 1', function () {});
test('Test 2', function () {});

// Second module
module('2nd module');
test('Test 1', function () {});
```

The `setup()` method is quite useful when you need to instantiate an object (such as a view or a collection) that will be used in multiple tests. The `teardown()` method, on the other hand, is mostly used to clean up the resources that you added as global variables.

Testing Backbone.js components with QUnit

Now as we understand the basics of `QUnit`, let's try it with some Backbone components. We will first start with a Backbone model and we will create a simple `User` model, as shown in the following code:

```
var User = Backbone.Model.extend({
  defaults: {
    name: 'Swapan Guha',
    age: 56
  }
});

module('User model tests', {
```

```
setup: function () {
    this.user = new User();
    this.user.set('age', 62);
  }
});

test('Can be instantiated with a default name and age to be set'
  , function () {
  equal(this.user.get('name'), 'Swapan Guha');
  equal(this.user.get('age'), 64);
});
```

Here, we tested the Backbone model with one of its default values and another attribute that we changed in the `setup()` method, but intentionally tested it with another value. So, this test should fail for one assert case. The following screenshot shows how it will look in a browser:

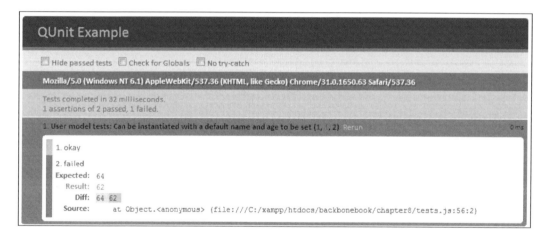

Using test spies, stubs, and mocks with SinonJS

We use unit testing to test one component of an application. That component can be a function, an object, a variable, or any outcome which is not known yet, and your unit test wants to make sure whether that particular component is working fine or not. Often, besides testing separate components, you may find testing the behavior of your methods is of the same importance. For example, how many times a method is called, what it returns, whether it has thrown any exception, what arguments it is called with, and so on. To perform these types of behavioral testing, we use test spies, stubs, and mocks.

There are few testing libraries which support test spies, stubs, and mocks. However, we found `SinonJS` quite easy to work with and robust as well. `SinonJS` works seamlessly with `QUnit` and you can use it with or without `QUnit` too. The definition of `SinonJS`, as given on their website, is as follows:

Standalone test spies, stubs and mocks for JavaScript. No dependencies, works with any unit testing framework.

Testing with spies

We first need to know what a spy is. By definition, as given on the `SinonJS` website, a spy is as follows:

A test spy is a function that records arguments, return value, the value of this and exception thrown (if any) for all its calls. A test spy can be an anonymous function or it can wrap an existing function.

So your next question should be why a spy should be used. We use test spies to test the behavior of callback and other methods, and to understand how they work. You will find out the answer in more detail once you look into some API methods associated with spies:

- `called()`: This returns true if the spy was called at least once
- `calledOnce()`: This returns true if the spy was called exactly once
- `returned()`: This returns true if the spy returned the provided value at least once

These are few of the supported methods of the spy API. Hopefully, now you can understand why a spy is used — it allows you to test multiple characteristics of a function, to know whether it gets called only once, or to check what value it returns. A spy allows you every possibility to test the complete flow of a function. Now let's see how to use a spy from the following code snippet:

```
// A User model definition
var User = Backbone.Model.extend({
  defaults: {
    name: ''
  },

  // Split the name to provide an array of first and last name
  getNameAsArray: function () {
```

```
      return this.get('name').split(' ');
    }
  });

  test('should call getNameAsArray and return an array',
      function () {
    this.user = new User({
      name: 'Krishnendu Saha'
    });

    // Added a spy on the the "getNameAsArray" method
    sinon.spy(this.user, 'getNameAsArray'); // or this.spy()
    this.user.getNameAsArray();

    // We check whether the method is called only once
    ok(this.user.getNameAsArray.calledOnce);

    // We check whether the returned value of this
    // method is an array
    equal(_.isArray(this.user.getNameAsArray.returnValues[0]),
      true);
  });
```

We used the same `User` model and added a `getNameAsArray()` method to it. We spied on this method to test whether it gets called only once and returns an array. The previous test case passes fine.

So, you can use spies for any or all of the following cases:

- Check for the invocation of a callback
- Validate whether callbacks are executed with certain arguments
- Validate if internal functions provide the correct return value
- Validate a certain simple calling behavior

Testing with stubs

A test stub, on the other hand, extends from a spy and adds some extra functionality to it. It is a function with preprogramed behavior and supports the complete spy API. It is used to replace (or fake) the behavior of an existing method with something. It is quite useful when you want to prevent a specific method from being called directly, or force a method to throw an error in order to test error handling. Like spies, stubs can either be anonymous, or they can wrap the existing functions. When wrapping an existing function with a stub, the original function is not called.

An anonymous stub can be defined as follows:

```
var stub = sinon.stub();
```

As a wrapper to a method of an object, it can be defined as follows:

```
var stub = sinon.stub(object, "method");
```

Here the function `object.method` is replaced with an anonymous stub function. You can also add one more function as the third parameter to the `stub()` function, which will work as a spy on `object.method` and will replace the original method as follows:

```
var stub = sinon.stub(object, "method", function(){});
```

To understand how a spy works with a real example, we can use the same `User` model that we previously used. This is shown in the following code snippet:

```
// We will use the same User model definition here

module("Should work when getNameAsArray method is called", {
  setup: function () {
    this.user = new User();

    // Use a stub to replace the getNameAsArray method
    this.userStub = sinon.stub(this.user, "getNameAsArray");
    this.userStub.returns([]);
  },

  // Restore the original method
  teardown: function () {
    this.userStub.restore();
  }
});

test('should call getNameAsArray and must return an empty array',
  function () {
  this.user.getNameAsArray();

  // Should return an empty array
  equal(_.isArray(this.user.getNameAsArray.returnValues[0]),
  true);
  equal(this.user.getNameAsArray.returnValues[0].length, 0);
});
```

Here, we stub the `getNameAsArray()` method of the `User` model and return an empty array. So while you call the `getNameAsArray()` method, *not the method but the stub will get called*. We made sure that the stub returns an empty array.

Now the test is as simple as the one we did earlier. We just call the `getNameAsArray()` method on the `User` instance and check the length of the returned value.

Testing with mocks

> *Mocks (and mock expectations) are fake methods (like spies) with pre-programmed behavior (like stubs) as well as pre-programmed expectations. A mock will fail your test if it is not used as expected.*

This is the definition of mock as given in the `SinonJS` website (`http://sinonjs.org/docs/#mocks`). Mocks are quite similar to stubs, but they come with built-in expectations. They implement both the spy and stub APIs. With a mock, you define all the expectations that should happen in your test. When all those things are done, you assert whether those things happened exactly the way they were planned. So you define the expectations and if they aren't met, the test fails.

Now, how do we use a mock? We mock an object, set expectations on its methods, and apply modifiers on these expectations. Then we verify whether the test passes all the expectations or not. To understand it better, let's explore a simple example with mock, as shown in the following code snippet:

```
test('should call getNameAsArray once and check it is called on the
user model', function () {
  this.user = new User({
    name: 'Subodh Guha'
  });

  var mock = sinon.mock(this.user);

  // We set the expectations here
  mock.expects('getNameAsArray').once().on(this.user);

  // Execution happens here
  this.user.getNameAsArray();

  // Now we verify whether the expectations are met or not
  mock.verify();
});
```

We use the same `User` model here and create a mock with a `User` instance. Then we set the expectation on the mock to see whether the `getNameAsArray()` method is called only once on that `User` instance. All these expectations are set beforehand and we verify them all together at the end.

Difference between mocks and stubs

Now, because stubs and mocks are similar in functionality, you may wonder why and when you should use a mock instead of a stub. As given by the website, you would use a mock only when you want to provide both alternate functionality and an expectation in your test. The main difference you can see is as follows:

- Mock objects are used to define expectations, that is, in a particular scenario, we expect the `Foo()` method to be called with a set of parameters. Mock records and verifies such expectations that whether the `foo()` method actually got called with those parameters or not.

- Stubs, on the other hand, have a different purpose—they do not record or verify expectations, but rather allow us to "replace" the behavior and the state of the "fake" object in order to utilize a test scenario.

To test the life cycle with stubs, proceed with the following steps:

1. Set up data: Prepare the object that is being tested and its stubs collaborators.
2. Exercise: Test the functionality.
3. Verify state: Use asserts to check the object's state.
4. Teardown: Clean up the resources.

To test the life cycle with mocks, proceed with the following steps:

1. Set up data: Prepare object that is being tested.
2. Set up expectations: Prepare expectations in a mock that is being used by the primary object.
3. Exercise: Test the functionality.
4. Verify expectations: Verify that correct methods have been invoked in the mock.
5. Verify state: Use asserts to check the object's state.
6. Teardown: Clean up the resources.

As you can see, there are pre and post states for a mock. We set the expectation before the test and verify it afterwards. Anyway, the purpose of both stub and mock is to eliminate testing all the dependencies of a class or function so that your tests are more focused and simple in what they are trying to prove.

Summary

We have included a number of books and tutorials related to QUnit and SinonJS in the *Appendix A, Books, Tutorials, and References*. You can follow them to get a more detailed idea about these two technologies.

A few testing concepts were described in this chapter. You got an idea about the power of QUnit and SinonJS, and how to use them extensively to unit test your JavaScript application. Though that barely scratches the surface, we never intended to cover everything about testing in this book either. We just tried to make you aware of the fact that testing is an absolutely important part of the application development process, and you should make it a habit to write test cases whenever you develop. It will make your code more structured, flexible, and easier to use for your teammates.

A
Books, Tutorials, and References

Backbone.js has an excellent documentation that provides a detailed overview of all of its components. However, you may find it insufficient to learn everything about the technology when you start developing your own applications. Throughout this book, various resources have been mentioned for different topics. I am listing a few more resources here. I found them to be very helpful while working with Backbone.js and recommend you to follow them too.

Books for reference

A large number of books on Backbone.js are available for beginners and advanced-level developers. However, the following three books, I believe, are a must-have for any Backbone.js developer:

- *Developing Backbone.js Applications, Addy Osmani*: This is the best book if you are a beginner and want to start learning Backbone.js. It covers almost everything about Backbone.js. Addy has an online version of the book too—you can find it in the following *Tutorials* section.

- *Building Backbone Plugins, Derick Bailey*: This is an excellent book where Derick talks about plugin development, the different problems with Backbone.js components, and their solutions.

- *Backbone.Marionette.js: A Gentle Introduction, David Sulc*: This book discusses the different components of the Backbone.Marionette extension along with detailed examples.

Tutorials

You will find a lot of tutorials online. I am listing a few of them; these are highly recommended and widely followed by developers:

- *Developing Backbone.js Applications* by *Addy Osmani* (`http://addyosmani.github.io/backbone-fundamentals/`)

- Blog posts by *Derick Bailey* (`http://lostechies.com/derickbailey/`)

- *Patterns For Large-Scale JavaScript Application Architecture* by *Addy Osmani*:
  - `http://addyosmani.com/largescalejavascript/`
  - `https://speakerdeck.com/addyosmani/large-scale-javascript-application-architecture`

- *Scalable JavaScript Application Architecture* by *Nicholas Zakas* (`http://www.youtube.com/watch?v=vXjVFPosQHw`)

- If you are a beginner, you may find the Backbone tutorials pretty helpful to understand the initial concepts (`http://backbonetutorials.com`)

Unit testing

The QUnit and SinonJS documentation provides complete details on test frameworks. The following are a few books and tutorials that you may find handy to help you master these frameworks:

- *Unit Testing Backbone.js Apps with QUnit and SinonJS* by *Addy Osmani* (`http://addyosmani.com/blog/unit-testing-backbone-js-apps-with-qunit-and-sinonjs/`)

- *QUnit Cookbook* by the *jQuery Foundation* (`http://qunitjs.com/cookbook/`)

- *SinonJS* by *Christian Johansen* (`http://cjohansen.no/talks/2011/xp-meetup/#1`)

- *Unit Test like a Secret Agent with Sinon.js* by *Elijah Manor* by *Elijah Manor* (`http://www.elijahmanor.com/unit-test-like-a-secret-agent-with-sinon-js/`)

Other plugins and tutorials

Apart from the previously mentioned resources, the Backbone.js wiki provides an updated list of the important plugins and tutorials, some of which are as follows:

- Backbone plugins and extensions at `https://github.com/jashkenas/ backbone/wiki/Extensions,-Plugins,-Resources`.

- Tutorials, blog posts, and example sites at `https://github.com/ jashkenas/backbone/wiki/Tutorials,-blog-posts-and-example- sites`.

- A number of Backbone.js plugins listed by popularity at `http://backplug.io/`.

- Backbone-Debugger at `https://github.com/Maluen/Backbone-Debugger`. This is a Chrome browser extension and can be helpful while working with Backbone applications. A similar Firebug extension can also be found at `https://github.com/dhruvaray/spa-eye`.

B

Precompiling Templates on the Server Side

In *Chapter 2*, *Working with Views*, we learned the advantages of using precompiled templates in your application. In addition, we saw a number of options to store your templates as inline in the `index.html` file or as separate template files. We also saw how we can use a template manager to precompile and cache templates to avoid compilation overhead every time. However, this precompilation process will run anyway when you start your application, which will surely take a certain period of time. Wait! Aren't these templates static resources? Then the compiled versions of the templates without data will also be static resources. Right? Then why not keep a separate file with all of the precompiled templates ready and use it as soon as your application starts? If you get a file with all of your templates already precompiled and minified, it will certainly boost your application's performance. This is what we will try here — we will develop a script to precompile the templates on the server side, which will traverse all of the template files and create a single template manager file. We use Node.js here, but you can use any server-side technology to get the same result. The complete working code is given in our code samples.

To precompile, we need a template engine with precompilation support. We will use Underscore.js here, but you are free to use your desired template engine to achieve the result. The following Node.js example shows you how to achieve this functionality:

```
// load the file system node module
var fs = require('fs'),
  // load the underscore.js
  _ = require('../../../lib/underscore.js');

var templateDir = './templates/',
  template,
```

```
    tplName,

    // create a string which when evaluated will create the
    // template object with cachedTemplates
    compiledTemplateStr = 'var Templates = {cachedTemplates : {}};
\n\n';

    // Iterate through all the templates in templates directory
    fs.readdirSync(templateDir).forEach(function (tplFile) {

        // Read the template and store the string in a variable
        template = fs.readFileSync(templateDir + tplFile, 'utf8');

        // Get the template name
        tplName = tplFile.substr(0, tplFile.lastIndexOf('.'));

        // Add template function's source to cachedTemplate
        compiledTemplateStr += 'Templates.cachedTemplates["' + tplName + '"]
= ';
        compiledTemplateStr += _.template(template).source + '\n\n';
    });

    // Write all the compiled code in another file
    fs.writeFile('compiled.js', compiledTemplateStr, 'utf8');
```

The preceding code is pretty self-explanatory. We created a complete JavaScript snippet as a string that will be returned to the frontend. Here are the steps to do so:

1. First, we browse through each template file in the `templates` directory and retrieve their contents.

2. We already have an object `Templates.cachedTemplates` defined and we need to store each template file's contents in this object with the template filename as a property and the template string as its value.

3. Underscore's `_.template()` method, in general, returns a function. It also provides a property called `source` that gives the textual representation of that particular function. The following line will give you the function source code:

   ```
   _.template(template).source
   ```

4. We place all of the function strings inside `Templates.cachedTemplates` one by one, and once the loop is over, we write the entire contents to another JavaScript file.

Now assume that the client side is asking for the `templates.js` file that contains the complete template content of the project. On the server side, we can write the following code that will send the `compiled.js` file content to the browser:

```
// While templates.js file is loaded, it will
// send the compiled.js file's content
app.get('/templates.js', function (req, res) {
  res
    .type('application/javascript')
    .send(fs.readFileSync('compiled.js', 'utf8'));
});
```

So, a request to the `template.js` file on the client side will display content similar to the following code:

```
var Templates = {
  cachedTemplates: {}
};

Templates.cachedTemplates["userLogin"] = function (obj) {
  var __t, __p = '',
    __j = Array.prototype.join,
    print = function () {
      __p += __j.call(arguments, '');
    };
  with(obj || {}) {
    __p += '<ul>\r\n     <li>Username:\r\n            <input type="text"
value="' +
      ((__t = (username)) == null ? '' : __t) +
      '" />\r\n     </li>\r\n     <li>Password:\r\n            <input
type="password" value="' +
      ((__t = (password)) == null ? '' : __t) +
      '" />\r\n     </li>\r\n</ul>\r\n';
  }
  return __p;
}
```

The final output is the `TemplateManager` object with the template's filename as its property and the compiled version of the template as the value of that property. This way, all of your template files will get added to the `TemplateManager` object. However, for this piece of code, you need to make sure that each template's filename is different. Otherwise, the template of the files with the same name will get overwritten by another.

You do not need to understand this compiled template function definition, as this will be used internally by the library. Be assured that once you call this function with the data object, you will get the proper HTML output:

```
var user = new Backbone.Model({
  username: 'hello',
  password: 'world'
});

// Get the html
var html = Templates.cachedTemplates.userLogin(user.toJSON());
```

This solution for precompiling JavaScript templates is very effective and you can use the same concept freely in your projects. We have used this concept in multiple projects successfully.

C
Organizing Templates with AMD and Require.js

Asynchronous Module Definition (AMD) is a JavaScript API used to define modules and load module dependencies asynchronously. It is a fairly new yet very robust concept that many developers are adopting nowadays. In *Chapter 7, Organizing Backbone Applications – Structure, Optimize, and Deploy*, we covered AMD with Require.js in detail. If you need more details on this library, we recommend you visit http://requirejs.org/ to get a complete overview and then come back to this section.

In general, Require.js treats every file's content as JavaScript. So, we cannot load our template files, if they aren't JavaScript files, in the same manner as JavaScript files. Fortunately for templates, there is a text plugin that allows us to load text-based dependencies. Any file that we load using this file will be treated as a text file and the content that we receive will be a string; it can be used easily with your template methods. To use this plugin, just prepend text! to the file path and the file contents will be retrieved as plain text; to do this, follow this example:

```
// AMD Module definition with dependencies
define([
    'backbone',
    'underscore',

    // text plugin that gets any file content as text
    'text!../templates/userLogin.html'
],
function (Backbone, _, userLoginTpl) {
    'use strict';

    var UserLogin = Backbone.View.extend({
```

```
      // Compile the template string that we received
      template: _.template(userLoginTpl),
      render: function () {
        this.$el.html(this.template({
          username: 'johndoe',
          password: 'john'
        }));

        return this;
      }
    });

    return UserLogin;
  });
```

The benefit of using this mechanism is that you can organize your templates by creating separate template files and they are automatically included in your modules. Since this involves asynchronous loading, the files are downloaded via AJAX requests, something we already decided as being a bad idea. However, Require.js comes with an `r.js` optimization tool that builds the modules and can save these extra AJAX requests by inlining these templates with their respective modules.

Precompiling with the requirejs-tpl plugin

With AMD, we simplified the template organization process, but the end result still remains an uncompiled template string. In *Chapter 2, Working with Views*, we saw how template compilation affects application performance every time and we also analyzed the benefits of precompiling templates. Won't it be useful if we have something that will load these template files and provide us with an already-compiled template string instead? Fortunately, there are multiple `tpl` plugins available for Require.js that automate template compilation, and you can use these plugins directly in your module definition. Let us look at a similar plugin (https://github.com/ZeeAgency/requirejs-tpl) developed by ZeeAgency. Dependency loading is exactly the same as it is for the `text` plugin, you just need to use the `tpl!` plugin prefix instead of `text!`:

```
define(['tpl!your-template-path.tpl'], function (template) {
  return template ({
    your: 'data'
  });
});
```

Now, `r.js` provides optimized and packaged precompiled templates. The `tpl!` plugin is surely more handy and useful than the `text!` plugin.

Template organization with Require.js is one of the best ways to maintain templates; a lot of JavaScript developers are opting for it nowadays. If you are using AMD for your Backbone application, go for it without any hesitation.

Index

error handler 123
event dispatcher
 about 98
 issues 99
 multiple event dispatchers, creating 99
 naming convention 100
expect() method 128
exports config 112

F

fetch() method 61, 75
findWhere() method 78
functional mixins
 creating 17, 18
 mixin functions, caching 18

G

getNameAsArray() method 132
getUserDetails() method 120
getView method 55

I

initialize() method 28, 35
isPrime() method 128
ItemView
 about 43-45
 close() method 43
 functionalities 43
 serializeData() method 43

J

JavaScript mixins
 about 15
 classic mixins, creating 16, 17
 functional mixins, creating 17, 18
JavaScript models 57
join() method 38

L

Layout Manager
 about 50
 serialize() method, using 52
 UserDetails view 51

UserItem view 51
UserList view 51
 using 50-55
listenTo() method 28
 used, for memory management 100, 101
ListItemView class 16
loadEvents() method 120
Lo-dash library
 about 11
 URL 11
loggedin event 98

M

Marionette
 about 43
 CollectionView 45
 CompositeView 46
 ItemView 43
 URL 43
memory management
 about 100, 123
 listenTo() method, using 100, 101
 memory leaks, avoiding with listenTo()
  method 100
mixin 16
Mocks
 differenciating, with Stubs 135
 testing with 134, 135
model data, views
 displaying, with templates 27
models, Backbone. *See* Backbone models
module() method, QUnit 129
multiple event dispatchers
 creating 99
multiple filtering
 disadvantage 80
multiple model types
 filtering 82
multiple routers 123

N

nested views
 about 29-32
 subviews, using 32, 33

O

offline storage
Backbone.LocalStorage adapter, used 104
online tutorials
unit testing 138
on() method 28

P

paths config 112
plugins
about 139
developing, without extending
base classes 14, 15
precompilation process 141
preValidate() method
used, for prevalidating model 66

Q

QUnit
about 126
Backbone components, testing 129
basic test case, performing 128
module() method 129
setup() method 129
teardown() method 129
URL 126, 127

R

relational data model 69
remove() method 101
render() function 27
require.config() method 112
Require.js
about 145, 146
adding, to application 111
properties 112
URL 111
requirejs-tpl plugin
about 146
used, for precompiling 146, 147
routers
about 85
best practices 87
working with 86

S

save() method 61, 75
serialize() method 52
set() method 75
setModel() method 55
setup() method, QUnit 129
setView() method 53
shim config 112
showChangedAddress() method 29
showUserName() method 31
sort() method 76
spies
testing with 131, 132
startDrag() method 20
stubs
testing with 132, 134
subrouter
about 90
all-in-one router 90
base router 91
users module router 92
subrouting 90
subviews
about 32
multiple DOM reflow, avoiding 33, 34
parent views, removing 35
parent views, re-rendering 34
using 32, 33

T

teardown() method, QUnit 129
template compilation 39
template helper functions
using 41, 42
templates
precompiling, on server side 141-143
templates, views
about 37
evaluation, avoiding 40, 41
precompiling 39
storing, in HTML file 37, 38
storing, in JavaScript file 38, 39
template helper functions, using 41, 42
Test Driven Development (TDD) 126
toJSON() method 58
tutorials 138

Thank you for buying
Backbone.js Patterns and Best Practices

About Packt Publishing

Packt, pronounced 'packed', published its first book "*Mastering phpMyAdmin for Effective MySQL Management*" in April 2004 and subsequently continued to specialize in publishing highly focused books on specific technologies and solutions.

Our books and publications share the experiences of your fellow IT professionals in adapting and customizing today's systems, applications, and frameworks. Our solution based books give you the knowledge and power to customize the software and technologies you're using to get the job done. Packt books are more specific and less general than the IT books you have seen in the past. Our unique business model allows us to bring you more focused information, giving you more of what you need to know, and less of what you don't.

Packt is a modern, yet unique publishing company, which focuses on producing quality, cutting-edge books for communities of developers, administrators, and newbies alike. For more information, please visit our website: www.packtpub.com.

About Packt Open Source

In 2010, Packt launched two new brands, Packt Open Source and Packt Enterprise, in order to continue its focus on specialization. This book is part of the Packt Open Source brand, home to books published on software built around Open Source licences, and offering information to anybody from advanced developers to budding web designers. The Open Source brand also runs Packt's Open Source Royalty Scheme, by which Packt gives a royalty to each Open Source project about whose software a book is sold.

Writing for Packt

We welcome all inquiries from people who are interested in authoring. Book proposals should be sent to author@packtpub.com. If your book idea is still at an early stage and you would like to discuss it first before writing a formal book proposal, contact us; one of our commissioning editors will get in touch with you.

We're not just looking for published authors; if you have strong technical skills but no writing experience, our experienced editors can help you develop a writing career, or simply get some additional reward for your expertise.

Backbone.js Testing

ISBN: 978-1-78216-524-8   Paperback: 168 pages

Plan, architect, and develop tests for Backbone.js applications using modern testing principles and practices

1. Create comprehensive test infrastructures

2. Understand and utilize modern frontend testing techniques and libraries

3. Use mocks, spies, and fakes to effortlessly test and observe complex Backbone.js application behavior

4. Automate tests to run from the command line, shell, or practically anywhere

Instant Backbone.js Application Development

ISBN: 978-1-78216-566-8   Paperback: 64 pages

Build your very first Backbone.js application covering all the essentials with this easy-to-follow introductory guide

1. Learn something new in an Instant! A short, fast, focused guide delivering immediate results

2. Structure your web applications by providing models with key-value binding and custom events

3. Keep multiple clients and the server synchronized

4. Persist data in an intuitive and consistent manner

Please check **www.PacktPub.com** for information on our titles

Made in the USA
Lexington, KY
26 March 2014